The Daily Telegraph

TAX GUIDE 2003

PREPARED BY
David B. Genders, F.C.A.
A partner of Sayers Butterworth, Chartered Accountants

MACMILLAN

First Published as *The Daily Telegraph Guide to Income Tax 1974*
27th edition, completely revised, published 2003 by Macmillan
an imprint of Pan Macmillan Ltd
Pan Macmillan, 20 New Wharf Road, London N1 9RR
Basingstoke and Oxford
Associated companies throughout the world
www.panmacmillan.com

ISBN 0 333 90678 0

Copyright © Daily Telegraph 1974, 2003

Every effort has been made to provide an up-to-date text but the publishers cannot accept any liability for errors, omissions or changes in detail or for any consequences arising from the use of information contained herein.

Please note that no reference is intended to actual individuals.

ACKNOWLEDGEMENT

The Inland Revenue forms reproduced in this book are Crown copyright and are reproduced with the permission of the Controller of Her Majesty's Stationery Office.

All rights reserved. No part of this publication may be reproduced, stored in or introduced into a retrieval system, or transmitted, in any form or by any means (electronic, mechanical, photocopying, recording or otherwise) without the prior written permission of the publisher. Any person who does any unauthorized act in relation to this publication may be liable to criminal prosecution and civil claims for damages.

1 3 5 7 9 8 6 4 2

A CIP catalogue record for this book is available from the British Library.

Printed and bound in Great Britain by
Mackays of Chatham PLC, Chatham, Kent

This book is sold subject to the condition that it shall not, by way of trade or otherwise, be lent, re-sold, hired out or otherwise circulated without the publisher's prior consent in any form of binding or cover other than that in which it is published and without a similar condition including this condition being imposed on the subsequent purchaser.

CONTENTS

Introduction, vi

1 You and the Inland Revenue, 1
Tax offices, The Collector of Taxes, Communicating with the Inland Revenue, Determinations, Enquiries, Assessments and appeals, Prosecutions, The Service Commitment, Complaints, Changes in legislation, Income Tax rates for 2002/03

2 Personal Allowances and Tax Credits, 9
Personal allowance, Married couple's allowance, Age allowances – Income limit, Blind person's relief, Children's Tax Credit, Other Tax Credits, Tax Credits from April 2003

3 Interest Payments and Other Outgoings, 16
Home annuity loans, Let property, Business loans, Gift Aid, Gifts of Assets to Charities, Payroll giving, Relief on life assurance premiums

4 Earnings from Employment, 21
Code numbers, How tax is worked out using your tax code, Forms P60, Changing your job, Expenses, Employee travel, Working from home, Benefits-in-kind, Employee share ownership, Enterprise Management Incentives, Payments on termination of employment

5 Value Added Tax, 39
Rates of VAT, Registration, Penalties for late registration, Help from Customs, Records and accounting, Input tax, Motor cars and fuel, Special schemes for retailers, Second-hand goods schemes, Helpful schemes for smaller businesses, Bad debts, Partial exemption, Routine compliance checks, Penalties, surcharges and interest, Supplies to/from EU countries, Appeals, Complaints

6 The Self-Employed, 51
Am I self-employed?, Starting up in business, Records, Accounts, Standard accounting information, Adjustment of profits, The current-year basis of taxation, Post-cessation expenses, Capital allowances, Losses, The Enterprise Allowance, Taking on an employee, Special situations

7 National Insurance Contributions, State Social Security and Insured Benefits, 65
National Insurance Contributions, State Retirement Pensions, Social Security Benefits, Insured benefits

8 Personal Pensions, 71
Eligible individuals, Benefits on retirement, Deferred annuities, Tax relief on premiums, Retirement annuities, Personal pension planning

9 Investment Income, 78
Tax-free income, Rental income, Rent-a-Room, Dividends and interest, Accrued income, Offshore funds, Overseas investment income, Non-qualifying life policies, Individual Savings Accounts, Tax-Exempt Special Savings Accounts, Personal Equity Plans, Friendly Societies, Enterprise Investment Scheme, Venture Capital Trusts, Joint income

10 The Family Unit, 91
Marriage, Children, Separation and divorce, Old age, Death

11 The Overseas Element, 96
Domicile, Residence and ordinary residence, Calculating annual average visits, Working abroad – long absences, Working abroad – expenses, Leaving the UK permanently, Allowances for non-UK residents, Income from UK property, Double taxation relief, Going abroad – Capital Gains Tax, Taking up UK residence

12 Capital Gains Tax, 102
Rate of tax, Married couples, Losses, The computation of gains, The indexation allowance, Taper relief, Assets owned on 31 March 1982, Quoted stocks and shares, Unquoted investments, Assets held on 6 April 1965, Valuations, Your private residence, A second home, Chattels, Wasting assets, Part disposals, Business assets, Enterprise Investment Scheme, Venture Capital Trusts, Gifts, Deferred gains on business assets and gifts, Inheritances

13 Completing the Return and Calculating your Tax, 126
Keeping proper records, Completing the Return, Calculating your tax, What the Inland Revenue does

14 Tax Payments, Interest, Surcharges and Penalties, 145
Tax payments, Statements of Account, Paying your tax, Date of payment, Interest, Remission of tax, Surcharges, Penalties

15 Elections and Claims – Time Limits, 152

16 Inheritance Tax, 156
Potentially exempt transfers, Gifts with reservation, Lifetime gifts, Exemptions, Business property, Agricultural property, Trusts, Rates of tax, Sales at a loss, Returns, Payment of tax, Legacies, Intestacy

17 Tax-Saving Hints, 164
Self-Assessment, Allowances and reliefs, Your job, Value Added Tax, Sole traders, Pensions, Tax-favoured investments, Capital Gains, Your home, Miscellaneous, Inheritance Tax

Tables, 174

1. Inland Revenue Explanatory Booklets
2. Flat-Rate Allowances for Special Clothing and the Upkeep of Tools – 2002/03
3. VAT Notices and Leaflets
4. Rates of National Insurance Contributions for 2002/03
5. National Insurance Explanatory Leaflets
6. Social Security Benefits
7. Rates of Main Social Security Benefits for 2002/03
8. Scope of Liability to Income Tax of Earnings
9. Capital Gains Tax – The Indexation Allowance: April 1998
10. Main dates of the Self-Assessment calendar

2003 Budget Measures, 185

INTRODUCTION

The Daily Telegraph Tax Guide is updated each year to reflect changes in:

- tax rates;

- allowances; and

- legislation.

This particular edition of the *Guide* is primarily intended to deal with the Self-Assessment tax system for 2002/03 and is being published at about the time you should be receiving a Tax Return asking for information about your income, capital gains, allowances and reliefs for the year ended 5 April 2003.

The Guide covers:

- Income Tax;

- Capital Gains Tax;

- Value Added Tax;

- Inheritance Tax;

- National Insurance and Social Security.

The changes in legislation enacted in the 2002 Finance Act are incorporated within this revised edition. The major proposals on taxation announced by the Chancellor in his Budget this April, which do not come into operation until after 5 April 2003, are set out in the supplement at the end of the book.

How can you benefit from reading the *Daily Telegraph Tax Guide 2003*? It has been written to assist you in:

- understanding and looking after your tax affairs with the minimum of difficulty;

- minimizing the amount of tax you pay;

- identifying tax saving hints and opportunities.

I hope the book is of interest and benefit to you.

1

YOU AND THE INLAND REVENUE

Before we look at the different types of taxable income and the various allowances and reliefs you can claim, I thought it would be helpful to give you an outline of the functions of the Inland Revenue departments which operate our tax system. Overall authority for administering the legislation enacted by Government is vested in the Board of Inland Revenue. Although there are a significant number of specialist departments within the Inland Revenue it is likely that your only direct contact with the Revenue will be through your tax office and the Collector of Taxes.

Tax offices
There are many tax offices spread out all over the country. Each office is headed up by a District Inspector with a full support staff of Inspectors and Clerks. If you are either employed or a pensioner, your tax affairs will be looked after by the tax office which deals with the Pay-As-You-Earn affairs of your employer or his pension fund. Where you are self-employed you will find that your local tax office is responsible for your tax affairs.

Over recent years, the Inland Revenue has been engaged in a fundamental reorganization of the local network of tax offices. In the present structure there are the following types of office:

Taxpayer Service Office (TSO)

It is your TSO which sends you a Tax Return to complete each year. The same office processes your Return when you send it back. If any obvious or simple errors come to light you can expect to receive a notice from the TSO detailing the amendments that have been made to your Tax Return. If you are late sending in your Return you can initially expect to be chased up by your TSO. Providing you comply with all your tax obligations it is unlikely that you will have any involvement with the Inland Revenue other than through your TSO.

TSOs look after all the day-to-day tax matters of the many taxpayers whose income is taxed under Pay-As-You-Earn and whose tax affairs are unaffected by the system of Self-Assessment. In addition, they are responsible for processing the business accounts of self-employed taxpayers.

Tax District Office (TDO)

In many parts of the country the local TDO is in the same office block as the TSO. Apart from providing technical assistance to the local TSO the TDO is responsible for:

- the investigation of the Tax Returns and business accounts of those taxpayers selected for further attention;
- enforcement and recovery action against you if you are late in paying your taxes or there is a prolonged delay in filing your Tax Return.

Complex Personal Returns (CPR)

Wealthy taxpayers with complex Tax Returns are now likely to find that they will be dealing with one of the Inland Revenue's new CPR teams. Taxpayers affected will receive a letter:

- telling them what is happening; and
- advising them of the name and telephone number of their 'personal case owner'.

It is likely that the Tax Returns of these taxpayers with large employment, Trust or foreign income will be more closely scrutinized leading to a higher level of enquiries.

Tax Enquiry Centre

The functions of a Tax Enquiry Centre are to:

- help with enquiries and provide assistance personally or over the telephone;
- accept payments of tax from taxpayers who prefer to pay locally;
- supply forms and leaflets.

The address and telephone number of your nearest Tax Enquiry Centre are in your local telephone book under Inland Revenue.

The Collector of Taxes

There are two Inland Revenue Accounts Offices. One is situated in Shipley, West Yorkshire, and the other is in Cumbernauld, Glasgow. Their job is to:

- bank payments of Tax and National Insurance Contributions; and
- keep up-to-date and accurate payment records.

If you need help you can telephone or write to either office. You should always quote your reference number.

Communicating with the Inland Revenue

On any straightforward matter where it helps you to have a quick answer it is better to telephone your tax office. Unless you specifically ask to speak to the Inspector you will be put through to one of his assistants who will usually be able to answer an enquiry about any of the following:

- General questions about Income Tax and Capital Gains Tax.
- Specific questions affecting your own liability to Income Tax.
- Help with completing Tax Returns and other Inland Revenue forms.
- Requests for leaflets, forms and other Inland Revenue information.

For individuals who prefer to do business with the Inland Revenue by telephone, the following services are available to taxpayers calling the tax office which handles their tax affairs:

- Personal details such as changes of address or personal circumstances.
- Employment details.
- Claims to personal allowances.
- Claims for relief for flat-rate expenses (see Table 2 on page 176) to be included in a PAYE coding for the current year.
- Employee benefits such as a company car, fuel for private motoring and medical insurance which affect your PAYE coding.

In most cases nothing more will be needed from the taxpayer, although the call may lead to further action by the Inland Revenue (for example, sending out a revised PAYE Coding Notice). Where business cannot be completely dealt with on the telephone the Inland Revenue officer will arrange for any necessary forms or follow-up material to be sent to the taxpayer.

On more complex aspects of your tax affairs I suggest you write to the tax office. Always remember to quote your reference number in any correspondence. This will be:

- your employer's PAYE reference; or
- your National Insurance Number; or
- if you are self-employed or pay tax at the higher rate, your Self-Assessment Unique Taxpayer Reference (UTR). This is a 10-digit number followed by the letter 'K'.

There may be times when a particular matter concerning your tax affairs can best be resolved by a detailed discussion. This is the time to arrange a visit to your tax office. Where this is situated a long way from your place of employment or home you can always arrange to go to any local Inland Revenue office or your nearest Tax Enquiry Centre.

Determinations

As may be expected, the Inland Revenue has special powers to deal with taxpayers who have been sent a Return but fail to submit it by the filing date. In such circumstances the Inland Revenue can make a determination to the best of their knowledge and belief of an offending taxpayer's income and capital gains chargeable to tax. The actual amount of tax owing is worked out after taking into account estimates of:

- the taxpayer's allowances and reliefs;
- tax deducted at source on earnings and savings income.

Any determination can be superseded at a later date by a self-assessment whether this be by the taxpayer or by the Inland Revenue based on information provided by the taxpayer. Until then the determination counts as a self-assessment.

Enquiries

When your Return is received by your tax office it will be processed and then subjected to a comprehensive programme of checks. If there are any obvious errors in your return, for example in your arithmetic, these will be corrected by your tax office and no further enquiries will probably be made of you. But enquiries will be started if:

- your tax office thinks something requires fuller explanation;
- the Inland Revenue think there is a risk your Return may be incorrect;
- your Return is picked for enquiry at random.

Normally the Inland Revenue have 12 months from the filing date for your Return in which to tell you that it will be the subject of enquiries. A longer period of time is allowed if you send in your Return late. At the end of that period, if there have been no enquiries, your Return will normally become final. The Inland Revenue can then only reopen the matter if they discover an error which they could not reasonably have been expected to be aware of from the information provided in, or with, your Return.

At the end of an enquiry into your Return the Inland Revenue will tell you what has been discovered and its effect upon your self-assessment Return. You will also be advised of the additional tax payable by you or of any refund which might be due to you. You then have 30 days in which to amend your self-assessment. If you do not accept the Inland Revenue's offer to alter your own self-assessment your Inspector of Taxes does have the powers to make the amendment.

Enquiries by local tax offices should be conducted in accordance with the specific Code of Practice laid down by the Inland Revenue. This might be an occasion when you should exercise your right to be represented by a professional advisor.

Assessments and appeals

There are two circumstances, related to fraud or neglect, when your Inspector of Taxes can raise an assessment to collect tax which should have been paid on a self-assessment.

You do, of course, have a right of appeal to the Commissioners against:

- an amendment to your Return; or
- an assessment raised by your Tax Inspector.

The procedure for resolving your appeal starts with a hearing before the General or Special Tax Commissioners. It can then move on to the Courts and ultimately to the House of Lords.

Prosecutions

An important role of the Inland Revenue is to deter fraud and the Inland Revenue will prosecute in serious cases in all areas of the tax system.

Cases selected for prosecution involve a wide range of offences but a case is more likely to be considered for prosecution if it contains features such as:

- falsification of documents;
- lying during an investigation;
- conspiracy;
- discovery of false documents made during an earlier investigation.

The Service Commitment

The standards of customer service to which the Inland Revenue is dedicated are laid down in its Service Commitment, the text of which is as follows:

The Inland Revenue is committed to serving your needs well by

acting fairly and impartially

We

- treat your affairs in strict confidence, within the law
- want you to pay or receive only the right amount due

communicating effectively with you

We aim to provide

- clear and simple forms and guidance
- accurate and complete information in a helpful and appropriate way

providing good quality service

We aim to

- handle your affairs promptly and accurately
- be accessible in ways that are convenient to you
- keep your costs to the minimum necessary

- take reasonable steps to meet special needs
- be courteous and professional

taking responsibility for our service
- we publish annually our customer-service aims and achievements
- if you wish to comment, or make a complaint, we want to hear from you so we can improve our service. We advise you how to do this.

we can provide better service if you help us by
- keeping accurate and up to date records
- letting us know if your personal/business circumstances change
- giving us correct and complete information when we ask for it
- paying on time what you should pay

Complaints

The starting point for any complaint should be the tax office with which you are dealing. Address your letter to the Officer in Charge, describe the complaint (slow service, constant mistakes) and the remedy you want (an apology, compensation).

Most complaints about the Inland Revenue's handling of people's tax affairs are satisfactorily settled by the local tax office concerned. Where taxpayers are not satisfied with the response from the local office, they can complain to:

- senior local management;

- the Inland Revenue's head office;

- a Member of Parliament;

- the Parliamentary Commission for Administration.

Taxpayers who are not satisfied with the Inland Revenue's response to their complaints also have the option of putting their case to the Inland Revenue Adjudicator. Complaints normally go to the Adjudicator only when they have been considered by senior local management and if the taxpayer is still not satisfied with the response he or she has received. The Adjudicator will review all the facts and aim to reach a decision as speedily as possible. Unless there are very exceptional circumstances the Inland Revenue will normally accept the Adjudicator's decision.

The Adjudicator will consider complaints about the way in which the Inland Revenue has handled someone's tax affairs – for example, complaints about excessive delay, errors, discourtesy – or the way in which the Inland Revenue has exercised discretion. The Board of Inland

Revenue receives an annual report from the Adjudicator which serves as a useful mechanism for identifying areas where problems are occurring and where changes may need to be considered.

Changes in legislation

Every year, the Chancellor of the Exchequer makes his annual Budget Statement. Not only does the Chancellor choose the occasion to introduce new or amending legislation to our tax laws, but he also announces the rates of tax and allowances for the following year.

The changes in legislation necessary to implement the Chancellor's proposals are subsequently published in a Finance Bill. The clauses in the Bill are debated and amendments are often proposed to some of them. Subsequently, the Bill is passed by both Houses of Parliament and receives the Royal Assent. It is then republished as a Finance Act.

It is the fiscal legislation passed by Parliament which is administered by the Inland Revenue. On occasions when the law is either unclear or ambiguous the Inland Revenue publish a Statement of Practice showing how they intend to interpret it. There are times when the Inland Revenue do not seek to apply the strict letter of the law. These are published as a list of Extra-Statutory Concessions.

The Inland Revenue also publish a number of booklets on different aspects of our tax system. A list of the most helpful booklets is set out in Table 1 at the end of the book.

Income Tax rates for 2002/03

Under our tax system, the tax (or fiscal) year runs from each 6 April to the following 5 April.

The rates of tax for 2002/03 are:

Band of Taxable Income	Rate of Tax	Tax on Band	Cumulative Tax
£	%	£	£
0 – 1,920	10	192.00	192.00
1,921 – 29,900	22	6,155.60	6,347.60
over 29,900	40		

The rate of 10% is known as the starting rate. The basic rate is 22% and tax at 40% is referred to as the higher rate.

Savings income, apart from dividends, is generally taxed at:

- 20% on income above the £1,920 starting rate limit but below the basic rate limit of £29,900; and
- 40% above the basic rate limit.

Income from UK dividends is taxed at:

- 10% on dividend income within the basic rate limit of £29,900; and
- 32.5% above the basic rate limit.

The law provides that the bands of income taxable at the starting and basic rates are to be increased each tax year in line with the movement in the Retail Prices Index during the year to the end of September prior to the tax year. The Treasury can, however, order an increase different to the statutory commitment, providing Parliament agrees.

2

PERSONAL ALLOWANCES AND TAX CREDITS

Every taxpayer with an income from earnings or investments is entitled to claim the personal allowance, ensuring at least some income each year is free of tax.

The rates of the various personal allowances for 2002/03 are:

		£
Personal	– (age under 65)	4,615
	– (age 65–74)	6,100
	– (age 75 and over)	6,370
Married Couples	– (born before 6 April 1935 and aged less than 75)	*5,465
	– (age 75 and over)	*5,535
	– (minimum amount)	*2,110
Children's Tax Credit		*5,290
Children's Tax Credit	– (baby rate)	*†10,490
Relief for Blind Person	– (each)	1,480

*indicates allowances where tax relief is restricted to 10%.

† in the first year of a child's life for babies born after 5 April 2002 and includes the Children's Tax Credit.

There is a page in your Tax Return for you to claim the particular allowances to which you are entitled. The allowances on which tax relief is unrestricted are deducted from your total income in calculating the amount on which you pay Income Tax each year. Tax relief for the other allowances, highlighted by an asterisk in the above table, is given as a deduction from tax payable.

The rates of allowances tend to vary from year to year. This is because the law provides that the allowances in the table above are to go up at the beginning of each tax year. This upwards movement is in line with the increase in the Retail Prices Index during the year to the end of September prior to the tax year. The Treasury can, however, order an increase different from the statutory commitment providing Parliament agrees.

Personal allowance

Every man, woman or child, single or married, resident in the UK is entitled to the personal allowance. This is set against their total income on which Income Tax is payable such as:

- a wage, salary or business profits;
- income from investments;
- an occupational and/or a state pension.

PERSONAL ALLOWANCES AND TAX CREDITS

Illustration

During 2002/03, Simon East, a married man, earned £20,000. His tax liability for the year is £3,154.30 as follows:

	£
Salary	20,000
Less: Personal allowance	4,615
Taxable income	£15,385
Income Tax Payable:	
£ 1,920 @ 10%	192.00
£13,465 @ 22%	2,962.30
	£3,154.30

A pensioner whose income is below a specified annual limit is entitled to a higher personal allowance: this is known as the personal age allowance. To be eligible, the elderly taxpayer must be aged 65 years or over for part or all of the tax year. There is a higher age allowance for a pensioner aged 75 or over for part or all of the tax year.

Married couple's allowance

A married man whose wife is living with him, can claim the married couple's allowance so long as one spouse was at least 65 years old on 5 April 2000. The amount of the married couple's allowance depends on the age of the elder spouse.

Illustration

Albert White was 70 years old in 2002/03. His wife, Joan, enjoyed her 62nd birthday the same year. They are entitled to allowances of £11,565 and £4,615 as follows:

	Albert	Joan
	£	£
Personal age/personal	6,100	4,615
Married couple's	5,465	–
Total allowances	£11,565	£4,615

Another elderly couple, Frank and Jean Barrett, had their 73rd birthday (Frank) and 77th birthday (Jean) in 2002/03. Their total allowances are £11,635 and £6,370 as follows:

MARRIED COUPLE'S ALLOWANCE

	Frank £	Jean £
Personal age	6,100	6,370
Married couple's	5,535	–
Total allowances	£11,635	£6,370

In the year of marriage the amount of the married couple's allowance depends upon the time during the year that the marriage took place. The allowance is reduced by one-twelfth for every complete month from 6 April up to the date of the wedding.

Illustration
Percy Hughes, aged 71, married his wife, Barbara, aged 67, on 13 July 2002. He receives an allowance of £4,099 for 2002/03 calculated as follows:

	£
Married couple's allowance	5,465
Less: Reduction $3/12 \times £5,465$	1,366
2002/03 Allowance	£4,099

The married couple's allowance is not reduced in the year when couples separate, divorce, or in the year of death of either spouse. A widow gets the benefit of any unused married couple's allowance in the year of her husband's death.

A wife can elect to receive £1,055 of the married couple's allowance. She does not need her husband's consent to make this election. Alternatively, £2,110 of the total allowance can be deducted wholly from the wife's total income, instead of the husband's income. This sort of election must be made jointly by husband and wife. In either situation the allowance to which the husband is entitled is reduced accordingly.

An election:

- must be made on the special Inland Revenue form 18;
- must normally be made before the beginning of the tax year for which it is to have effect (except in the year of marriage where a notice can immediately be given in respect of the reduced married couple's allowance for that year);
- once made applies for that year and each succeeding tax year until altered by subsequent election or notice of withdrawal;

- withdrawal is not effective until the tax year after that in which notice of withdrawal is given to the Inland Revenue.

If none of these elections is made, the husband is entitled to the full married couple's allowance. Where he has a sufficiently low taxable income and cannot make full use of his married couple's allowance he can transfer any excess allowance to his wife. Alternatively, if, following an election, a wife does not have sufficient taxable income against which to set off her part of the married couple's allowance she can transfer the excess back to her husband.

Age allowances – Income limit

As the personal age and married couple's allowances are designed to help those pensioners who are less well off, they reduce where their income before tax rises above £17,900 for 2002/03. This reduction in age allowances is one-half of the amount by which total income exceeds the stated limit of £17,900, although it cannot take the rate of the allowance below the level of either the personal allowance or a married couple's allowance of £2,110, as the case may be. The personal age allowance is reduced before the married couple's allowance.

Income for this purpose is after taking off:

- pension contributions paid; and

- donations under Gift Aid.

Whether an elderly spouse can claim the personal age allowance depends solely on the amount of his or her income. However, any restriction of the married couple's allowance is measured solely by the husband's income. It is never affected by the amount of the wife's income.

Illustration

Another elderly couple, James Flowers, aged 79, and his wife Betty, aged 69, whose income amounted to £13,000 and £19,000 respectively during 2002/03 are entitled to allowances of £11,905 and £5,550 as follows:

	James £	Betty £
Income before tax		
State pensions	3,926	2,350
Pensions from former employers	5,074	9,650
Investment income	4,000	7,000
	£13,000	£19,000

Allowances		
Personal age	6,370	6,100
Married couple's	5,535	–
	£11,905	£6,100
Less: Reduction		
½ × £1,100 (£19,000 – £17,900)	–	550
2002/03 Allowances	£11,905	£5,550

It follows that no measure of personal age allowance is due to an elderly taxpayer (aged 65–74) whose income exceeds £20,870 for 2002/03. For a pensioner aged 75 or over the maximum income limit is increased to £21,410.

The upper income limits for a husband beyond which no measure of married couple's allowance is due for 2002/03 are:

	Wife's Age	
Husband's Age	*65–74	Over 74
	£	£
Under 65	24,610	24,750
*65–74	27,580	27,720
Over 74	28,260	28,260

* Born before 6 April 1935

The income limit for age allowances goes up each tax year in the same way as the main personal allowances.

Blind person's relief

This relief is given to a registered blind person. Where both husband and wife are blind they may each claim the relief. A husband or wife who is unable to use up his or her blind person's relief fully because of insufficient income, can transfer any unused part of the relief to the other spouse even if he or she is not blind.

When an individual first becomes entitled to the allowance, by being registered blind, the allowance will also be given for the previous year if, at the time, the individual had obtained the necessary proof of blindness required to qualify for registration. This prevents individuals losing out as a result of delays in the registration process.

Children's Tax Credit

You can claim the Children's Tax Credit if:
- you have a child living with you for at least part of the year; and

PERSONAL ALLOWANCES AND TAX CREDITS

- the child is under 16 years old at the start of the year; and
- the child is your own (including a step-child or an adopted child) or you look after the child at your own expense.

The maximum allowance for a household for 2002/03 is £5,290, increasing to £10,490 if a baby is born during the year. However, this is reduced if you pay tax at the 40% rate. Then the allowance comes down by £2 for every £3 of income taxed at 40%.

For couples the credit must be claimed by the person with the higher income.

Illustration
Paul and Carol Lane have three children, all under age 16. Paul is on an annual salary of £35,500. Carol earns £23,000 p.a. Paul must claim the Children's Tax Credit for the family as he is the higher rate taxpayer. Paul pays tax at 40% on £985 of his income as follows:

	£
Salary	35,500
Less: Personal allowance	4,615
Taxable income	£30,885
Income Tax Payable:	
£1,920 @ 10%	192.00
£27,980 @ 22%	6,155.60
£985 @ 40%	394.00
	£6,741.60

The tax credit which Paul can claim is reduced by £656 (2/3 × £985) to £4,634.

Providing neither of you pays tax at the top rate of 40%:

- you can both elect for the person with the lower income to have all the credit; or
- share the credit equally.

Whatever rate of tax you pay, you only get tax relief at 10% on your Children's Tax Credit. If you are employed this means that there must be a restriction of the allowances in your tax code to avoid an over allowance.

Illustration
Barry Cole is entitled to the maximum Children's Tax Credit for 2002/03 of £5,290. The allowances in his tax code for 2002/03 will be restricted by £2,885 worked out as follows:

	£
Tax relief on £5,290 @ 22%	1,163.80
Less: Relief due at 10%	529.00
Tax over allowance	£634.80

Restriction in tax code is £634.80 × $\frac{100}{22}$ =   £2,885.45

Other Tax Credits

The Working Families Tax Credit is payable at varying rates to families – either lone parents or couples (married or otherwise) – who:

- have one or more children;
- are resident, and entitled to work, in the UK;
- work at least 16 hours a week;
- have savings of £8,000 or less.

Likewise, the Disabled Person's Tax Credit is also payable at varying rates but to people with a disability or illness who:

- are resident, and entitled to work, in the UK;
- work at least 16 hours a week;
- have savings of £16,000 or less;
- qualify for certain disability benefits.

Tax Credits from April 2003

All the above three credits are replaced from 6 April 2003 by two new ones – the Child Tax Credit (CTC) and the Working Tax Credit (WTC). The main features of these new Social Security benefits are:

- The CTC and the childcare element of the WTC will be paid direct to the main carer, usually the mother, providing a secure and regular stream of income.
- The awards will be based on the income of the family so one- and two-earner couples on the same income will be similarly treated.
- For 2003/04 they will be calculated by reference to income in 2001/02.
- Where circumstances change during the year, for example a baby is born, you can ask for the amount of your claim to be adjusted.
- Claim forms should be completed before 6 July 2003 by everyone who might qualify, otherwise there may be some loss of entitlement to one or other of the new credits.

3

INTEREST PAYMENTS AND OTHER OUTGOINGS

As the opportunities to claim tax relief for interest paid on borrowed money are limited, you should be aware of the few occasions when you can do so. These are:

- the purchase, in certain circumstances, of life annuities if you are aged 65 or over;

- buying a share in

    - a partnership, or contributing capital to a partnership, if you are a partner;

    - a close company or lending capital to it;

    - an employee controlled company;

- buying plant and machinery for use in a job or partnership providing the plant and machinery attracts capital allowances for tax purposes.

It is important to appreciate that the purpose for which a loan is raised governs whether the interest on it will be eligible for tax relief. How the loan is secured is irrelevant.

Generally the interest on which tax relief is due is deducted from your total income in the year of payment. This general rule does not apply where you borrow money to buy a property which you let out: this is dealt with later on in the chapter.

Home annuity loans

Interest on loans taken out before 9 March 1999 to purchase an annuity from an insurance company still attracts tax relief at 23% providing:

- the borrower was at least 65 years old at the time the annuity was purchased;

- not less than 90% of the loan on which the interest is payable went towards buying an annuity for life;

- security for the loan is the borrower's main residence.

The maximum amount of the loan on which tax relief is allowed is

£30,000. If your loan exceeds the limitation of £30,000 you will receive tax relief on that part of the total interest payable equivalent to this limit. The 23% tax relief will be taken into account in arriving at the regular payments to be made to the lender.

Let property

Interest on a loan taken out to buy or improve a property which you rent out is tax deductible. The interest is set against the rental income from the property. Should the interest payable in a tax year exceed the rents receivable in the same year, the loss can only be carried forward to future years.

Illustration

Paul Green bought a property in 1992 with the assistance of an £80,000 loan. He lets it out and the rents less expenses came to £3,800 and £12,000 during 2001/02 and 2002/03 respectively.

	2001/02		2002/03
	£	£	£
Rents less expenses	3,800		12,000
Less: Loan interest paid	5,000	6,000	
Loss carried forward	£1,200	1,200	
			7,200
2002/03 Taxable Income			£4,800

Business loans

Most businesses need to borrow money at some time for one purpose or another. Interest on any such borrowings is allowable as a deduction against your business profits providing the borrowed money is used for business purposes. It does not matter for this purpose whether the borrowings arise because your bank account goes overdrawn, or because you take out a loan for some specific purpose connected with your business.

If you need to borrow to buy an asset – such as a car or a piece of machinery – for use in your business, the interest you pay will qualify for tax relief but will be restricted where the asset is also used privately.

If you are about to become a member of a partnership, you may need to borrow money to purchase a share in the partnership or to contribute capital for use in its business. Should that be the case, the interest on the borrowings will qualify for tax relief.

INTEREST PAYMENTS AND OTHER OUTGOINGS

Alternatively, you may have business connections with a private company. The interest on a loan raised so you can either acquire shares in the company or lend it money for use in its business will qualify for tax relief. You must either own at least 5% of the company's share capital or have at least some shareholding and work for the greater part of your time in the business.

Employees who need to borrow to buy shares in their company as part of an employee buy-out are allowed tax relief on the interest.

Gift Aid

Gift Aid is an Income Tax relief for cash gifts, without limit, by individuals to charities. Under Gift Aid a charity can reclaim back from the Inland Revenue the basic rate tax on your cash donation, thereby increasing the value of the gift to the charity. For example, a cash gift of £10 is worth £12.82 to a charity under Gift Aid.

You can:

- give any amount, large or small, regular or one-off;
- pay by cash, cheque, postal order, standing order, direct debit, or by using your credit or debit card.

For your donation to qualify under Gift Aid you must:

- pay at least as much tax in the tax year in which you make your cash gifts as the charities will reclaim on them;
- make a declaration to the charity that you want your donation to be regarded as made under Gift Aid.

If you pay tax at the top rate of 40% you can claim tax relief on the difference between the higher and basic rates of tax on all your Gift Aid payments.

Illustration

Norman Walton gave donations totalling £1,560 under Gift Aid in 2002/03. Norman is a higher rate taxpayer so he can reduce his tax bill by £360 as follows:

	£
Grossed up donations – £1,560 × 100 / 78 =	£2,000
Tax relief thereon at 40%	800
Less: Deducted when making donations	440
Reduction in Income Tax payable	£360

If you do not pay tax, Gift Aid is not for you.

Gifts of assets to charities

You can claim relief from Income Tax at your top rate of tax for the full market value of any gifts of shares, securities or land and buildings to charities at the time of the gift. The assets which qualify for this type of tax relief are:

- shares or securities listed on, or dealt in, a recognized Stock Exchange;
- units in an authorized unit trust;
- shares in an open-ended investment company;
- an interest in an offshore fund;
- land and buildings.

This Income Tax relief is in addition to exemption from Capital Gains Tax on such assets given to charities.

Illustration

Jennifer Pickard pays tax at the higher rate of 40% on a substantial part of her income. She decides to give shares in a quoted company valued at £5,000 to a registered charity. The taxable capital gain on the shares would be £3,000 if she sold them. Jennifer saves tax as follows:

	£
Reduction in Income Tax (40% x £5,000)	2,000
Capital Gains Tax not payable on the gain (40% x £3,000)	1,200
Maximum tax saving	£3,200

Payroll giving

If you are in employment there may be a further alternative way open for you to make donations to charity. This depends on your employer operating such a scheme through an Approved Agency Charity. Then your charitable donations can be made through your employer by way of regular deductions from your salary. Employers are not bound to launch such schemes and employees can choose whether to participate in them. Where you do so, you will be entitled to tax relief on your payroll donations to charity.

Relief on life assurance premiums

These days life assurance serves many purposes. They range from providing for the payment of lump sums on death, either to pay off the amount of an outstanding mortgage or to leave a lump sum for the deceased's dependants, to other uses which can often serve as tax-efficient forms of investment.

There are two kinds of life assurance policy for tax purposes, qualifying and non-qualifying policies. There are numerous conditions which must be satisfied if a life assurance policy is to count as qualifying. However, the life assurance office with which you are taking out a policy will have taken care of all these points. There is usually neither Income Tax nor Capital Gains Tax to pay on the maturity or claims value of a qualifying policy.

The amount of tax relief on premiums paid on qualifying life assurance policies is at the fixed rate of 12.5% on policies taken out before 14 March 1984. It should not be necessary for you to claim this since the premiums paid to the life assurance company are after deduction of the 12.5% tax relief. There are occasions when some or all of this relief can be withdrawn, and then a payment to the Inland Revenue will have to be made for the tax relief which has been lost. For example, the amount of such premiums which can be paid in any tax year without restriction of the tax relief is limited to £1,500 or one sixth of your total income before allowances, whichever is greater.

Illustration
Donald Kingsford pays annual qualifying life assurance premiums of £1,700 before tax relief. If his income is:

(a) £12,000, the 12.5% tax relief is unrestricted;

(b) £9,000, he will only receive the 12.5% tax relief on premiums of £1,500.

Premiums payable on a qualifying life assurance policy taken out after 13 March 1984 do not attract any tax relief. The same applies to future premiums payable on a similar policy taken out before that date if, after 13 March 1984, the benefits secured under the policy are varied or its terms extended.

4

EARNINGS FROM EMPLOYMENT

Most of you will be familiar with at least some part or other of the Pay-As-You-Earn (PAYE) system. It provides a mechanism for collecting the tax due on the earnings of those people in employment. Employers must deduct Income Tax from the earnings of their employees and every month the total of these deductions has to be paid over to the Inland Revenue. The PAYE taken off an employee's earnings is treated as a credit against the overall amount of tax payable by the employee for the tax year in question. In working out the amount of tax to deduct from each employee's salary or pay packet, the employer takes into account each individual's own allowances and other reliefs. This is possible because the Inland Revenue issue employers with a code number for each employee. In turn the code number incorporates each employee's allowances and reliefs. The system allows for these to be spread evenly throughout the tax year to avoid any substantial variation in the amount of tax deducted from each salary cheque or pay packet.

The sort of earnings which count as taxable income from an employment are:

An annual salary or wage
Bonus
Overtime
Commission
Tips or gratuities
Holiday pay
Sick pay
Earnings from a part-time employment
Directors' fees or other remuneration
Benefits-in-kind

All directors and employees are taxed on the earnings they actually receive in a tax year.

Code numbers

I have already mentioned that each employee is issued with a code number by the tax office. In theory the code number should ensure that the correct amount of tax has been deducted from your earnings by the end of the tax year. The system can only work properly and effectively if your local tax office is kept informed of any changes in your personal circumstances which affect the amount of your allowances or reliefs.

For example, most if not all notices of coding for the 2003/04 tax year commencing on 6 April 2003 were issued during the early part of the year. This is before taxpayers complete their year 2003 Tax Returns which require a report of each person's income, capital gains, reliefs and allowances for the tax year just finished – the year to 5 April 2003. It follows that the information on which all the code numbers for 2003/04 have been based is out of date. This is why it is important you should check your code number for 2003/04 and tell your Inland Revenue office if:

- any alterations are required to your allowances or reliefs;
- you start receiving a pension;
- there is a big change in your income;
- you change your address.

You may be surprised when you come to compare your code number for 2003/04 with that for the previous year. This is because the Chancellor has already announced that the personal and age-related allowances for 2003/04 will be:

	£
Personal	4,615
Age	
• Personal (age 65–74)	6,610
• Married couples (age 65–74)	5,565
• Personal (age 75 and over)	6,720
• Married couples (age 75 and over)	5,635

For 2003/04 the minimum amount of the married couple's allowance will be £2,150 and the income limit for age allowances goes up to £18,300.

If there are any other changes to tax rates and allowances in the spring 2003 Budget you will be sent details with any further coding notice issued to you for 2003/04.

On the following page is an illustration of a notice of coding for David Jones for 2003/04. David is a married man with two children under 16. He does not pay tax at the top rate of 40%. His allowance for 2003/04 is £4,615 before deductions as the Children's Tax Credit is no longer in his tax code (see Chapter 2). The first three of these deductions relate to benefits-in-kind in the form of a company car and private

CODE NUMBERS

PAYE Coding Notice

Tax code for tax year **2003/04**

MR D. JONES
79 ACORN STREET
FIELDGATE
TA6 2PY

Please keep all your coding notices. You may need to refer to them if you have to fill in a tax return. Please also quote your tax reference and National Insurance number if you contact us.

Issued by
T.G. MATTHEWS
H.M. INSPECTOR OF TAXES
FIELDGATE DISTRICT
FIELDGATE HOUSE
FIELDGATE
TA6 7DP

Tax reference: **195/F249**

National Insurance number: **FX 57 30 29 C**

Your tax code for the year shown above is **5 L**

This tax code is used to deduct tax payable on your income from
FIELDGATE TEXTILE CO LTD

If you move to another job, your new employer will normally continue to use this tax code. The tax code is worked out as follows:

The '**See note**' columns below refer to the numbered notes in the leaflet '**Understanding Your Tax Code**'. This tells you about the **letter part** of your tax code.

Check that your details are correct. If you think they're wrong, or you have any questions, ask me (my details are above).

This coding notice replaces any previous notice for the year.

See note	Your tax allowances	£
01	PERSONAL ALLOWANCE	4615
A	**Total allowances**	**4615**

See note	Amounts taken away from your total allowances	£
30	CAR BENEFIT	1500
30	CAR FUEL BENEFIT	2160
30	MEDICAL INSURANCE	400
39	TAX UNPAID	500
B	**Total deductions**	**4560**

C Your tax free amount for the year is £ **55**, making your tax code **5 L**   see example overleaf

Previous tax code

If necessary we will use this box to give you further information about your tax code

P2

62482 01.03 Guilbert UK   BS1/03   R0H1202

23

medical insurance cover provided by David's employer. Some of the types of taxable expenses and benefits are dealt with later on in this chapter. The coding notice illustrates how the tax payable on benefits-in-kind is usually collected. This is done by restricting David's allowances by the value of the benefits-in-kind which, in total, amount to £4,060.

The final deduction is for tax underpaid for 2001/02 of £110. For any one of a number of reasons the allowances given, or deductions made, in David's coding notice may subsequently turn out to be incorrect. If, as a result, there is an underpayment of tax, this is usually collected in a later year, again by restricting allowances in the coding. In our illustration a reduction in allowances for 2003/04 of £500 will result in the Inland Revenue collecting the underpayment of £110 (£500 @ 22%) from David during the year. A similar sort of adjustment to David's coding notice for 2003/04 will also be made if he sent his Tax Return for the year to 5 April 2002 back to his tax office by 30 September 2002 and asked to pay tax owing for the year (less than £2,000) through the PAYE system.

The combined effect of these adjustments is to leave David with allowances of only £55 to be set against his salary for 2003/04. His code number will be 5L. Clearly, there is a direct link between David's allowances and his code number. The suffix letter is added to the coding as a means of identifying the category into which a taxpayer falls. This is what the letters stand for:

- L – is for a code with the basic personal allowance;
- P – is for a code with the personal allowance for those aged 65–74;
- V – indicates the pensioner is entitled to both the personal and married couple's allowances for ages 65–74 and is liable to tax at the basic rate;
- Y – is the code if you are due the personal allowance for age 75 and over; and
- T – applies in most other cases, for example:
    - You ask your tax office not to use any of the letters listed above.
    - Where there are other items in the coding which need to be reviewed.

There are also a number of other codes:
- OT – no allowances have been given to you. Tax will be deducted at the starting rate, then the basic rate, and finally at the higher rate, depending on your income;

HOW TAX IS WORKED OUT USING YOUR TAX CODE

- BR – this is an instruction for your employer to deduct tax at the basic rate;
- NT – this means that no tax will be deducted;
- DO – tax will be deducted at the higher rate;
- Prefix K – a K code is given to employees whose taxable benefits exceed their personal allowances. The amount of the negative allowances is then added to the pay on which tax is to be paid. This system of K codes is designed to make taxpayers pay all the tax due on their benefits evenly throughout the tax year under the PAYE system, instead of receiving a demand at the end of the tax year for the lump sum owing.

How tax is worked out using your tax code

The coding notice issued to David Jones for 2003/04 tells him that his tax-free amount for the year is £50. He earns £21,000 per annum for his job.

Illustration
The deduction for tax is worked out as follows:

	£
Pay from employment	21,000
Less: tax-free amount for year	50
Tax worked out on	£20,950

	£
Income Tax payable	
£ 1,920 @ 10%	192.00
£19,030 @ 22%	4,186.60
	£4,378.60

To work out the weekly amounts of pay and tax, divide the pay and tax payable for the year by 52:

Weekly pay is £21,000 ÷ 52 = £403.85

Weekly tax is £4,378.60 ÷ 52 = £84.20

To work out the equivalent monthly amount divide by 12:

Monthly pay is £21,000 ÷ 12 = £1,750.00

Monthly tax is £4,378.60 ÷ 12 = £364.88

Forms P60

Shortly after the end of each tax year every employer sends to the Inland Revenue a Return summarizing the names of all employees, their earnings during the tax year and the deductions made for both Income Tax and National Insurance Contributions. By 31 May following the end of a tax year your employer must hand you a Form P60. This is a certificate of your earnings for the past tax year incorporating the Income Tax and National Insurance Contributions you paid. For most employees the Income Tax withheld under PAYE corresponds with the tax due on their earnings. Overleaf is an illustration of the Form P60 sent to David Jones by his employer for 2002/03. This shows that the tax deducted from his earnings in the year amounted to £3,870.80 based on a tax code of 238T. It also tells him that he suffered National Insurance Contributions of £1,646.40 in 2002/03.

Changing your job

Whenever you change your job your employer will hand you Parts 1A, 2 and 3 of a Form P45. This form details your name and address, the name and address of your employer, your tax district and reference number, and your code number at the date of leaving. It also shows your cumulative salary and tax deductions for the tax year up to the date that you leave, and your salary and tax deductions from the last employment unless this information is the same as the cumulative figures. Your employer will send the first part of the P45 form to his tax district.

You must hand Parts 2 and 3 of the Form P45 to your new employer. He will enter your address and the date you start your new job before sending Part 3 of the form to his own tax office. The information on the form enables your new employer to make the right deductions for Income Tax and National Insurance from your new salary or wage.

You should keep Part 1A of the form for your own records. If necessary, it can then be used to assist you in the preparation of your own tax return.

Should you not have a P45 to hand to your new employer, you will find that the deductions from your salary for Income Tax are equivalent to those of a single person without any other allowances or reliefs. This is known as the 'emergency' basis. Where this happens you should either ask for and complete a Tax Return or send in sufficient information to your new employer's tax office so that the correct code number can be sent to your employer. If you have just left school or are taking up employment for the first time you should complete either a Form P15 or a Form P46 as a way of making sure that the right deductions for Income Tax are made from your wage or salary.

CHANGING YOUR JOB

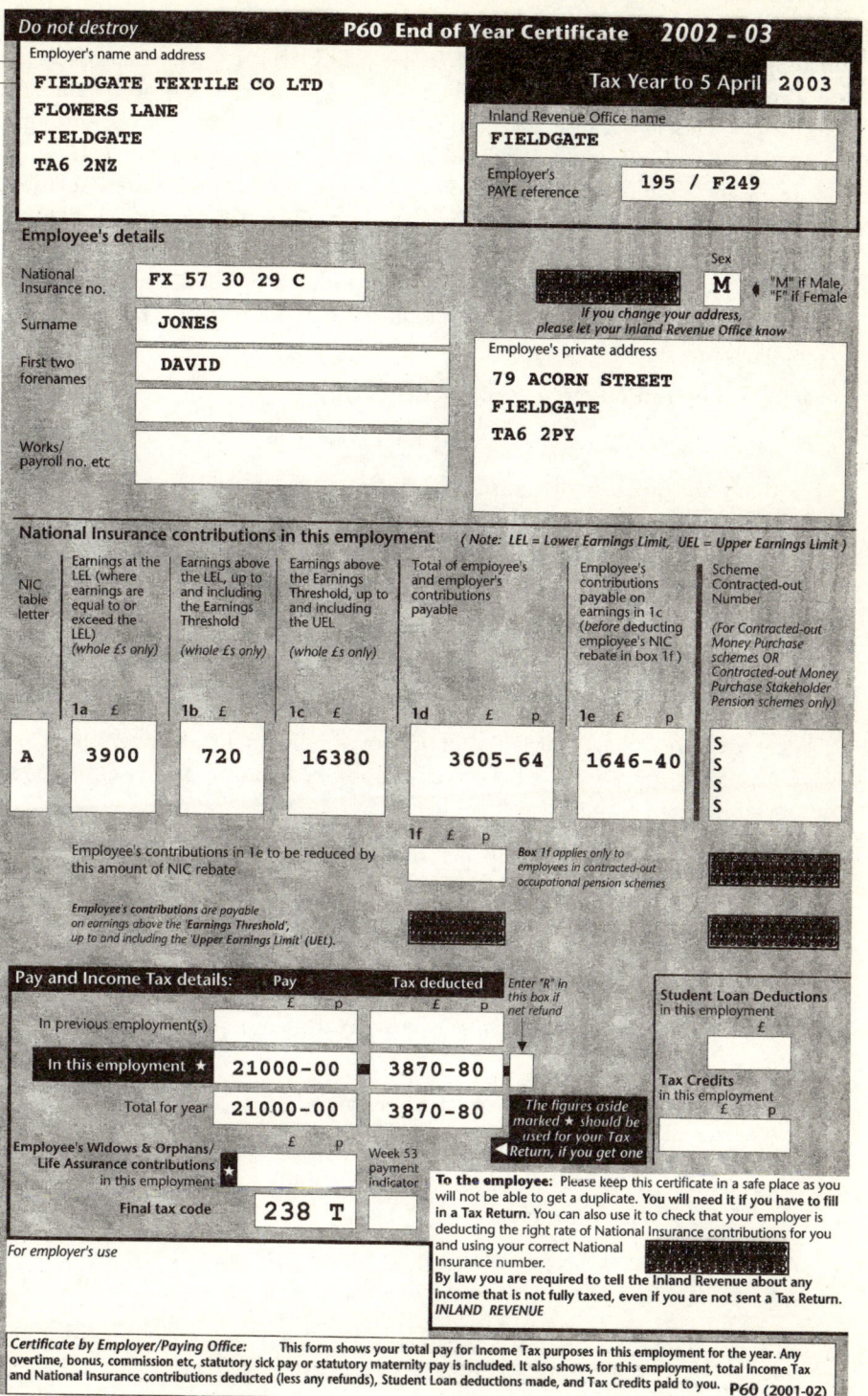

Expenses

The rules which allow you to claim tax relief on expenses relating to an employment are extremely restrictive. They seek to deny tax relief on almost all types of expenses which are not ultimately borne by the employer. This is because the employee has to show that any expenditure is incurred 'wholly, exclusively and necessarily' while performing the duties of the employment. If the employer has not been prepared to foot the bill for the expenditure involved, then the Inland Revenue are likely to take the view it was incurred more as a matter of choice than of necessity. Nevertheless, some business expenses paid personally are deductible from your income. Details of these should be entered on your Tax Return. They include:

- annual subscriptions to a professional body;
- business use of your own car and telephone;
- clothing and upkeep of tools – the Inland Revenue and the Trade Unions have agreed flat-rate allowances for the upkeep of tools and special clothing for most classes of industry. The current rates are set out in Table 2. As an alternative you may claim a deduction for the actual expenses on these items;
- payment by directors or employees for work-related insurance cover. Tax relief is also allowed on meeting the cost of uninsured liabilities.

Most expenses you incur in your job or employment are probably borne by your employer, who either reimburses you on an expense claim or pays for them direct. Tax-free for everyone are:

- luncheon vouchers up to 15p per day;
- free or subsidized meals in a staff canteen, providing the facilities can be used by all staff;
- sporting and recreational facilities;
- staff parties, providing the annual cost to the employer is no more than £75 per head;
- routine health checks or medical screening;
- computer equipment lent by employers providing the cash equivalent of the benefit does not come to more than £500 each year. Any excess over £500 remains taxable;
- awards for long service of at least 20 years. The cost of the articles purchased by the employer must not exceed £20 for each year of service;
- gifts not exceeding £150 in a tax year to an employee from a third party – by reason of his or her employment;
- out-placement counselling costs;

- child-care facilities at the work place or elsewhere (but not on domestic premises);
- parking facilities for cars, motorcycles or bicycles at or near your place of work;
- a works bus service;
- the cost of infrequent private transport when you have been working late and either public transport is no longer available or it would be unreasonable to expect you to use it at a late hour. Infrequent late working means a requirement to work until at least 9.00 p.m. not more than 60 times in a tax year;
- bicycle and cycling safety equipment made available to employees to get them between home and work;
- equipment or facilities provided to disabled people to enable them to carry out their job;
- mileage allowances where employees use their car, motorcycle or pedal cycle on business. The tax-free rates laid down by the Inland Revenue for 2002/03 are:

Cars and Vans
First 10,000 miles	40p per mile
Excess	25p per mile
Motorcycles	24p per mile
Bicycles	20p per mile

Employees are taxed on payments made by their employers over and above the rates in the table. But they can claim tax back on the difference where their employers pay them less than the permitted rate.

- personal incidental expenses when you stay away from home overnight on business. The most common expenses covered are newspapers, telephone calls to home, and laundry. The tax-free limits, including VAT, are £5.00 per night for overnight stays anywhere within the United Kingdom and £10 per night for overnight stays elsewhere. Where an employer exceeds these limits, the whole of the payment becomes taxable – not just the excess;
- contributions by your employer to your education or training if you are an Individual Learning Account (ILA) holder. Your employer must make contributions available to all employees on similar terms.

Employee travel

Tax relief is allowed on all business travel, where journeys start from home or from an employee's permanent workplace. The cost of travelling between home and work is not allowable for tax purposes, except for disabled employees who are given financial help by their employers with home-to-work travel on public transport or by some other means.

Where the full cost of an employee's journey is not reimbursed by the employer, the employee can claim tax relief on the excess miles not paid for by the employer.

(a) Site-based workers

'Site-based' workers are those employees who work at a number of different places for periods of a few weeks or months at a time. Their reimbursed travelling expenses are tax free providing:

- The worker initially expects the posting not to exceed two years; and the stay must actually last for less than this time.

- There is no stipulation for an employee to return to his or her permanent workplace when each site job comes to an end.

- An employee's work on site may be considered as a single continuous period even if he or she is occasionally moved off-site.

(b) Employees with areas

The geographical area covered by employees, such as salesmen, is treated as their permanent place of work. The following special rules apply:

- All travel within the area is considered to be eligible for tax relief.

- Where an employee lives outside his or her area, travel to the start of the area is classed as home-to-work travel and is taxable if paid for by the employer.

- The whole country is likely to be the area for any employee whose duties extend to servicing customers throughout the entire UK.

The entire travelling appointments of service engineers are treated as business travel eligible for tax relief.

(c) More than one workplace

No tax relief will be due for travel from home to either place of work for those individuals with more than one permanent place of location. It is the Inland Revenue's view that a workplace is likely to be considered as permanent if:

- An employee regularly performs 40% or more of the duties of his or her employment there.

- Customers, suppliers and others would expect to be able to make contact with the employee there.

- The employee has an office, or desk and support services.

Working from home

An ever increasing number of people are now giving up on the daily commute in favour of working from home, either full-time or on a part-time basis. This is made more possible because of modern technology.

But, to get tax benefits, you must be able to demonstrate that your working from home is necessary rather than by choice. If you satisfy this test you should be able to claim tax relief on:

- A proportion of your household costs such as heating, lighting, Council Tax and telephone.

- Use of your car, computer and tools for your employer's business.

- Other expenses you incur on stationery, books and professional subscriptions for the business.

Benefits-in-kind

Employees (including full-time working directors who own 5% or under of the company's shares) earning less than £8,500 per annum including expenses are not taxed on most benefits or perks provided by their employers. In addition to those in the above list, the most valuable non-taxable benefits for this type of employee are private medical insurance and a company car.

Other directors and employees (including full-time working directors), whose total earnings, including expenses, exceed £8,500 per annum, are generally taxed on the actual value of any benefits and taxable expenses obtained from their employments. Information about your expense payments and benefits-in-kind is supplied by your employer to your tax office annually on a Form P11D. Your employer is required to give you a copy of this form by 6 July following the end of the tax year.
It represents your employer's calculations of your taxable payments and cash equivalents of benefits-in-kind. It is down to you to justify those on which you should not be taxed. This should not cause you any difficulties where the expenses, such as travelling and entertaining, have genuinely arisen from the performance of the duties of your employment.

There are set rules for calculating some benefits.

(a) Company cars

The taxation of company cars has been substantially reformed from 6 April 2002. Under the new system:

- The tax charge continues to be based on a percentage of the list price of a car but graduated according to the level of the car's carbon dioxide (CO_2) emissions. The minimum charge is 15% of a car's price increasing to a maximum of 35% of list price if CO_2 emissions are above the prescribed level.

- The previous business mileage and car age discounts are abolished.

- Diesel cars are subject to a 3% supplementary charge in view of their higher emissions of pollutants. This measure does not, however, take the maximum charge above 35% of a car's price.

The car benefit charges for cars with an approved CO_2 emissions figure for the 2002/03 to 2004/05 tax years are as follows:

CO_2 emissions in g/km			% of list price which is taxed
2002/03	2003/04	2004/05	
165	155	145	15
170	160	150	16
175	165	155	17
180	170	160	18
185	175	165	19
190	180	170	20
195	185	175	21
200	190	180	22
205	195	185	23
210	200	190	24
215	205	195	25
220	210	200	26
225	215	205	27
230	220	210	28
235	225	215	29
240	230	220	30
245	235	225	31
250	240	230	32
255	245	235	33
260	250	240	34
265	255	245	35

Diesel Supplement

Add 3% up to a maximum of 35%

The new regime applies to all cars, not just new ones. However, special rules apply to older cars (those registered prior to 1 January 1998) which are taxed on a percentage of list price based on engine size:

Engine Size	% of List Price which is taxed
Up to 1,400	15
1,401 – 2,000	22
2,001 or more	32

Diesel Supplement

Add 3% for diesel cars

Mileage between your home and place of business counts as private, not business, usage except in a car made available by an employer where:

- the employee has a travelling appointment;

- the employee travels from home to a temporary place of work and the distance travelled is less than the distance between the normal place of work and the temporary place of work;

- exceptionally, the home qualifies under tax law as a place of work and the employee travels from home to another place of work in the performance of his duties.

There are also circumstances where home-to-work travel in a car provided by an employer is regarded as private use but is ignored for tax purposes. These are where:

- a disabled person is provided with a car for home-to-work travel and there is no other private use;

- a car is provided for home-to-work travel when public transport is disrupted;

- a car is provided for late-night journeys from work to home;

If it is the company's policy to meet the cost of fuel for private motoring there is an additional taxable benefit. Again, it is based on predetermined fixed amounts dependent on the cubic capacity of the company car. For 2002/03 the scale of benefits is:

	Engine Size	Fuel Benefit
	cc	£
Petrol	0 – 1,400	2,240
	1,401 – 2,000	2,850
	over 2,000	4,200
Diesel	0 – 2,000	2,850
	over 2,000	4,200
Cars without a cylinder capacity		4,200

From 6 April 2003 the car fuel benefit is based on £14,400 multiplied by the same percentage as that used to calculate the car benefit.

(b) Company vans

Also taxable on a fixed amount is an employee to whom a company van is made available for private use, again including travel between home and work. For 2002/03 the taxable benefit is £500 for a van under four years old at the end of the tax year. For an older van the amount on which you pay tax is reduced to £350. Both fixed benefits also cover the cost of any fuel provided for private motoring. These rules apply to a company van with a design weight up to 3,500 kilograms. There is no taxable benefit on the incidental private use of a heavy commercial vehicle with a design weight exceeding 3,500 kilograms.

(c) Pooled vehicles

The private use of a car or van from an employer's pool of vehicles will not give rise to a tax charge on an employee provided:

- Any home-to-work travel is merely incidental to business use.

- The vehicle is not garaged at or near the employee's home overnight.

(d) Living accommodation

In some trades it is established practice for the employer to provide living accommodation. This can also be desirable where there is a security risk. No Income Tax liability arises in either sort of situation.

In other circumstances Income Tax is chargeable on the annual value of the property after deducting any rent paid for it. The annual value of property for these purposes is broadly equivalent to the gross rateable value. Estimated rateable values will be used for new properties which do not appear on the domestic rating lists. An additional tax charge must be faced where the accommodation costs more than £75,000. This is worked out by applying the Inland Revenue's official interest rate (see below) at the beginning of the tax year to the excess of the cost price over £75,000.

(e) Beneficial loans

Loans from an employer which are either interest free or where the interest charged by the employer is below a commercial rate can give rise to a taxable benefit. The benefit is calculated by applying the Inland Revenue's official rate of interest to the loan. For the 2002/03 tax year the rate is 5.00%. The benefit is reduced by any interest actually paid on the loan. No charge to tax arises where all an employee's cheap or interest-free loans, excluding loans which qualify for tax relief, total no more than £5,000. A tax charge is also avoided where the loan is for a purpose on which the interest would qualify for tax relief (see Chapter 3).

(f) Medical insurance

You will be taxed on private medical insurance premiums paid by your employer for you or other members of your family. If you go abroad on business then the cost of medical insurance cover, or actual medical treatment overseas, is not taxable on you as a benefit.

(g) Relocation expenses

An employee who changes his job, or is relocated by his employer, is not taxed on the costs of a relocation package up to £8,000. This limit applies to each job-related move. There are specific definitions for the removal expenses and benefits which qualify for exemption within the monetary limit.

Employee share ownership

There are a variety of share, profit sharing and share option schemes, all offering different investment limits and tax reliefs – some more generous than others.

(a) Under an All-Employee Share Scheme:

- employers can give employees up to £3,000 of shares free of tax and National Insurance;
- some or all of these shares can be awarded to employees for reaching performance targets;
- employees are able to buy partnership shares out of their pre-tax salary or wage up to a maximum of £1,500 a year, free of tax and National Insurance;
- employers can match partnership shares by giving employees up to 2 free shares for each partnership share they buy;

- employees who sell their shares are liable to Capital Gains Tax only on any increase in the value of their shares after they come out of a plan;
- free and matching shares must normally be kept in the plan for at least three years – employees can take partnership shares out of the plan at any time;
- shares must come out of the plan when employees leave and some employees may lose their free and matching shares if they leave their jobs within 3 years of getting the shares;
- dividends, up to £1,500 annually, paid on the shares are tax free providing they are reinvested in additional shares in the company;
- employees who keep their shares in a plan for 5 years pay no Income Tax or National Insurance on those shares;
- employees who take their shares out of a plan after 3 years pay Income Tax and National Insurance on no more than the initial value of the shares – any increase in the value of their shares while in the plan is free of Income Tax and National Insurance;
- Capital Gains Tax roll-over relief is available for existing shareholders of smaller companies who want to sell their shares to a new plan trust to be used for the benefit of employees.

(b) The main features of a Savings-Related Share Option Scheme are:

- it operates in combination with either a bank or building society SAYE savings contract under which employees save a fixed regular amount each month;
- the maximum amount that can be saved is £250 per month over either a 3- or 5-year period;
- the price at which options can be offered to directors and employees cannot be less than 80% of the market value of the shares at the time the options are granted;
- the receipt of the options and any increase in the value of the shares between the time that the options are granted and the date when they are exercised are free of Income Tax.

(c) Under an Approved Profit-Sharing Scheme:

- a company makes an allocation of profits to Trustees who, in turn, use the contribution in acquiring shares in the company which are subsequently allotted to employees;
- the limit on the market value of shares which may be appropriated to any one individual in each tax year is 10% of salary with a minimum limit of £3,000 and a maximum of £8,000;

- there is no Income Tax liability when the shares are set aside nor if they are retained by the Trustees of the scheme for 3 years.

(d) Inland Revenue Approved Share Option Plan:

- no liability to Income Tax is imposed on a director or employee who acquires, or disposes of, ordinary shares under such a plan;
- the market value of shares, at the time of the grant of the option, over which an individual holds unexercised rights under the plan must not exceed £30,000;
- an option must be exercised not less than 3, or more than 10, years after it is granted, nor under 3 years after a previous exercise;
- the gain is measured by the difference between the sale proceeds and the cost of acquiring the shares, and is charged to Capital Gains Tax at the time of disposal;
- the price payable must be fixed at the time of the grant and must not be less than the market value of the shares at that date;
- options granted before 17 July 1995 under then approved schemes continue to qualify for tax relief on exercise even if they exceed the £30,000 ceiling now applying to company share option plans.

Enterprise Management Incentives

Enterprise Management Incentives have been designed to help small companies attract and retain the key people they need and to reward employees for taking a risk by investing their time and skills in helping small companies achieve their potential.

Companies can grant share options to employees worth up to £100,000 at the time of grant, normally without any charge to Income Tax or National Insurance. Moreover, when the shares are sold, Capital Gains Tax taper relief normally starts from the date when the options were granted.

A qualifying employee is one who must spend at least 25 hours a week or, if less, 75% of their working time, on the business of that company.

Payments on termination of employment

It is common practice for an employee to be paid a lump sum on the termination of an employment. If the right to receive the payment arose during the period of employment then it is taxable in full in the same way as other earnings. Otherwise the lump sum payment is either wholly or partly tax free. The occasions when the payments are free of tax are:

- where the employment ceases because of the accidental death, injury or disability of the employee;

- where most of the employee's time was spent working overseas for the employer;
- where the lump sum payment is made at a time other than on death or retirement. The first £30,000 is then tax free. Only the excess of any payment over £30,000 is taxable.

Any statutory redundancy payment you receive, although exempt from tax itself, has to be counted in with any other lump sum payment from your employer in working out the tax due on the lump sum.

Redundancy and employment termination settlements often provide for some benefits, such as membership of a company medical insurance scheme, to continue after termination. Such payments and benefits are taxed only to the extent they arise, and in the year in which they are received or enjoyed.

Illustration

Patrick Bond lost his job in July 2002. Under his employment termination settlement he received lump sum redundancy payments of £25,000 and £15,000 on 23 July 2002 and 16 April 2003 respectively. He was also allowed to remain a member of his employer's company medical insurance scheme for three years at an annual cost of £800.

Patrick's total redundancy package for 2002/03 comes to £25,800. As this is below the £30,000 exemption limit he does not pay tax on that part of the package he received and enjoyed in 2002/03. The £4,200 balance of the exemption limit is carried forward to 2003/04 to be set against the cash payment of £15,000 and the medical insurance benefit of £800. In 2003/04, therefore, Patrick's employer will deduct tax at the basic rate on £11,600.

5

VALUE ADDED TAX

Although Value Added Tax (VAT) applies throughout Europe, more and more countries outside the European Union are now adopting it as a system for taxing what people spend. After setting the level for the standard rate, governments are able to decide what areas of expenditure should qualify for relief, and how relief should be given. The tax can then be collected quite cheaply.

VAT is administered by Customs and Excise. There are VAT Business Advice Centres throughout the country. You can find the one nearest to you from the telephone directory. The main contact point for businesses nowadays is, however, the National Advisory Service (NAS) on telephone number 0845 010 9000. Calls are logged, and if you do have a query it is as well to ask for the reference number just in case you ever need to refer to it later on. If your enquiry happens to be of a technical nature, it is always recommended that the details are set out fully in a letter to the VAT Business Centre covering the area where your business is. A reply should be sent to you promptly.

Customs now have a wide range of publications on their website – www.hmce.gov.uk – and, if necessary, hard copies of any relevant material required can either be downloaded or obtained on request from the NAS.

Basically, VAT is a self-assessed tax on supplies made by businesses. The following paragraphs give those who are new to the tax, or who have little experience of it, an insight into some of the rules and more common problems. Also mentioned are the procedures Customs have introduced to help smaller businesses.

Rates of VAT

The majority of goods and services supplied in the UK are liable to tax at the standard rate of 17.5%. Among the broad areas where relief has been granted are:

- Zero rated supplies
    - Food sold in shops
    - Books and newspapers
    - Construction of new houses

Passenger transport
Exports of goods

- Supplies liable at 5%
    Domestic fuel and power
    Renovations and alterations of dwellings
    Residential conversions

- Exempt supplies
    Education
    Health and welfare
    Insurance
    Land
    Finance and banking transactions

It is important to realize that zero, 5% and 17.5% are all rates of tax, since the time for deciding whether, and, if so, when, to apply for registration depends upon the level of taxable supplies made. The income from any exempt supplies does not count towards the registration limit.

Registration

If your business is just starting, it is unlikely you will have to register immediately: only when the value of your taxable supplies reaches £55,000 in a 'rolling' period of 12 months is application compulsory.

It is vital that you do not delay submitting an application for registration as soon as it has to be made. The NAS will arrange for the issue of a VAT 1 Form to you. This has to be completed no later than 30 days from the end of the month after the one in which your turnover exceeds the £55,000 limit. Registration would then be effective from the beginning of the next month.

Illustration

Simon Potter commenced in business on 1 May 2002. Turnover in what would be taxable supplies reflected a steady increase to start with but then went up quite sharply towards the end of his first year as the following table shows:

REGISTRATION

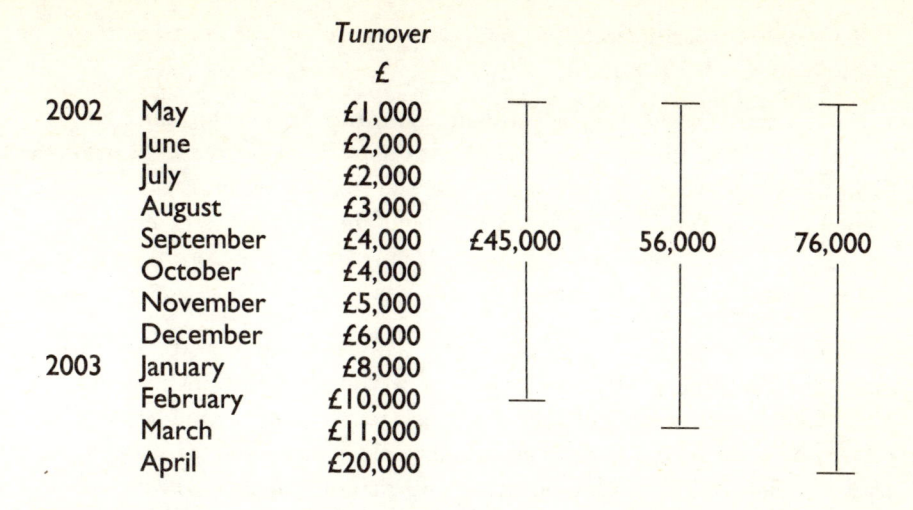

		Turnover			
		£			
2002	May	£1,000			
	June	£2,000			
	July	£2,000			
	August	£3,000			
	September	£4,000	£45,000	56,000	76,000
	October	£4,000			
	November	£5,000			
	December	£6,000			
2003	January	£8,000			
	February	£10,000			
	March	£11,000			
	April	£20,000			

As turnover in the period from 1 May 2002 to 28 February 2003 was less than £55,000 there was no requirement to register. Turnover did exceed the threshold at the end of March 2003 and registration had, therefore, to be applied for during April 2003. However, since the date from which registration would take effect would be 1 May 2003, tax would not have to be charged until then. This would mean that not only the supplies throughout the earlier part of the trading period but also during April, when in that month alone they totalled £20,000, would not have to bear tax.

There is no escape from registration unless Customs can be convinced that either

- there was expected to be a drop in taxable turnover so that, from then on, it would remain at an annual level of less than £53,000, or
- the business would be one where, if registration was in place, repayments of VAT would normally have to be made.

Requests not to be registered would, in these circumstances, normally be granted, provided that your VAT Business Centre was told afterwards of any changes which might alter the position.

Sometimes there are benefits in registering even though turnover does not come up to the compulsory registration limit. Voluntary registrations of this nature are allowed if you can show that you are, or will be, making some taxable supplies. In this way VAT incurred on your business expenses may be claimed back, including the VAT paid on assets like computers and printers on hand at the time of registration, as well as on certain business start-up costs.

If you are in partnership you must also complete a VAT 2 Form in addition to the VAT 1 Form.

Do not delay registering if you happen to buy an existing business, such as a shop, where the previous owner was already registered. The turnover build-up to £55,000 from the time you take on the business does not then apply: the turnover before you bought the business is taken into account as well. Sometimes it is possible for the registration number of the previous owner to be transferred to you.

Shortly after you have completed and submitted the registration forms, you should receive a letter advising you of your registration number. Your formal certificate will follow a week or two later. One or two notices or leaflets of a general nature may be sent to you with this correspondence. There may be more information which would be of interest to you and your business. Table 3 at the end of the book lists some of the VAT notices currently available. The NAS will, upon request, forward whatever you think that you need if you do not have the facility to access and obtain material from the Customs website.

Penalties for late registration

New businesses which do not keep an eye on how their turnover is progressing can be caught out by a scaled penalty imposed for not registering when they should. The penalty is calculated as follows:

Registration not more than nine months late	5%
Registration over nine months but not more than 18 months late	10%
Registration more than 18 months late	15%

The penalty is based on the net tax due for the period from the time registration should have started to the date the VAT 1 Form is received by Customs or liability to be registered is discovered. There is a minimum penalty of £50.

Payment of the back-tax has to be made as well of course although an arrangement to clear it in stages may be possible.

Help from Customs

As part of their revised policy Customs have said that they intend to make contact with new businesses by telephone within the first few months after registration. Assistance will be offered with any queries which may have already arisen, helpful videos offered to those businesses which may benefit from them, and the opportunity will be afforded either to attend a seminar or to have a one-to-one meeting to go into any matters of an individual nature. Simplification methods will also be discussed. You may find this particularly useful since this book only has space to touch on certain aspects.

It has also been announced that there will not be such a hard-line approach if a business, new to VAT and with a turnover below £150,000, faces initial problems with completing the first couple of VAT Returns, or paying the tax shown to be due. However, it has been made clear that any initial hiccups are expected to be only short-term: when businesses have been up-and-running for a while, they are expected to be better able to cope with VAT for themselves – especially with the NAS to fall back on for general guidance and help.

Records and accounting

Output tax is what you are liable for on the supplies you make (outputs) and input tax is on the purchases you receive (inputs). You should keep a copy of every invoice issued for supplies made by your business. It is recommended that an analysed listing should be made of them which at least includes the following:

Invoice		Customer	VAT excl Value	VAT	Gross Value	Date payment received
No	Date					
			£	£	£	

Similarly, and unless you have sought and been granted approval to use the Flat Rate Scheme (see the section *Helpful schemes for smaller businesses* on page 46) purchase invoices should be analysed in your records and filed by you in such a way that it is possible to trace any item where input tax is claimed to the tax invoice for the purchase.

Totalling your outputs and inputs monthly should make it fairly straightforward to bring together the details for the VAT accounting periods shown on your certificate of registration. A summary of the monthly tax totals can be noted in a VAT Account which acts as a link between your own records and the VAT Return – Form VAT 100 – which will be sent to you. If you are allocated quarters in line with the calendar quarters and you account for VAT on the basis of invoices raised and received, the VAT Account may, for the January to March period, be like this:

VALUE ADDED TAX

VAT Account Period 1 January 2003 to 31 March 2003

	£	£
Output Tax		
January	2,470	
February	2,360	
March	2,520	
Total	£7,350	7,350
Input Tax		
January	910	
February	820	
March	680	
Total	£2,410	2,410
Net amount due		£4,940

The figures in your VAT Account and the tax-exclusive values of your outputs and inputs will put you in a position to complete the various boxes on your VAT Return.

When the Return ends up showing an amount of tax payable to the Customs and Excise you should send it off and pay what is due. If the VAT claimable on the purchases for the business exceeds the VAT on the supplies you have made to customers or clients, the Return will show you are entitled to a repayment. It is likely this will be sent direct to your bank account although it may be subject to verification by your VAT Business Centre before you receive the refund.

You can request that your quarterly VAT Return periods are set to tie in with your financial year if you wish.

Input tax

It is only the input tax which is incurred on purchases for your business which can count towards how much is claimed. Sometimes you might incur expenses where the input tax cannot be claimed at all. Examples are business entertaining and private purchases paid for by your business. Occasionally there may be a need to apportion input tax such as that on home telephone bills, which are partly for business and partly for private purposes. Apportionment is best done on a percentage basis. Customs and Excise will go along with your method provided that it is reasonable.

Motor cars and fuel

Businesses which are directly concerned with motoring, like new car dealers, vehicle hirers, taxi drivers or driving schools, may be able to claim back in full the input tax on cars which they buy or lease. The input tax cannot be claimed on cars bought by other businesses and made available for private use. With car leases, however, it may be possible to claim 50% of the input tax on the rental payments.

As for motor fuel, most businesses choose between two basic ways for dealing with input tax. All input tax on the fuel may be claimed with a fixed-scale charge applied to take account of private use. Alternatively – and you should tell your VAT Business Centre if you intend to do this – no input tax is claimed and the fixed-scale charge is ignored. As a guide, claiming input tax and using the fixed-scale charge is normally the better way if private motoring paid for by the business is more than about 8,000 miles a year.

The quarterly scale charges are as follows:

Engine Size – cc	Diesel Scale Charge £	VAT £	Petrol Scale Charge £	VAT £
1400 or less	212	31.57	226	33.65
1401 to 2000	212	31.57	286	42.59
Over 2000	268	39.91	422	62.85

Input tax on repairs and maintenance of business cars can be claimed whichever way you decide to deal with motor fuel.

Special schemes for retailers

Retailers often sell a mixture of both positive- and zero-rated goods but do not know how much of each from day to day. When this happens they can use one of the schemes devised to help them work out their VAT liabilities. If your business falls into this category, you should study the leaflets telling you about the various schemes so that you do not pay too much tax.

Where retailers sell only goods which are liable to the standard rate of 17.5%, the amount of tax included in the gross takings for a period is $7/47$. Referred to as the 'VAT fraction', the basis for this calculation is as follows:

		£
Tax exclusive value (say)		100.00
Add: VAT @ 17.5%		17.50
Tax inclusive price		£117.50

The VAT included in the tax inclusive price is therefore:

$$\frac{17.5}{117.5} = \frac{7}{47}$$

For goods liable at 5% the 'VAT fraction' will be $\frac{1}{21}$. When retailers are asked for one, they must issue a proper tax invoice for supplies where the value exceeds £100. For supplies below this figure, till receipts will usually have enough information on them for the appropriate VAT fraction to be applied by customers who, in the course of their business, make retail purchases and want to claim back the input tax suffered.

Second-hand goods schemes

For many years there have been a number of schemes where certain types of business have had to keep detailed stock records. Using the 'VAT fraction' they have had to work out the tax to pay on an item-by-item basis according to how much the selling price exceeds the purchase price. In this way, the liability is just on the dealer's margin, no allowance being made if an item is sold at a loss. There is also a Global Accounting Scheme which makes it much easier for those businesses trading in large volumes of second-hand low-value goods to work out the tax. Although a values limit of £500 for an article has been set, a business which uses this scheme can take the overall margin in the whole of the tax period and apply the VAT fraction to it. An item-by-item calculation is unnecessary.

Helpful schemes for smaller businesses

(a) Cash Accounting and Annual Accounting

Available to businesses with a turnover up to £600,000 these schemes are optional. Cash Accounting allows businesses to account for tax just on the basis of what is actually received and paid. Annual Accounting, as the name implies, can be applied for by those businesses which have been registered and up-and-running for a year, have a satisfactory VAT 'history', and would prefer to render their VAT Returns on an annual, rather than a quarterly, basis. There is some leeway if turnover exceptionally exceeds the limit but care is needed if turnover is likely to stay that way. Apart from only having to submit one VAT Return each year there are other benefits from annual accounting, including:

- fewer declarations, therefore fewer deadlines and less risk of penalties;
- a reduction of some paperwork during the year, with an extra month to complete the annual return; and
- fixed interim payments that provide an aid to cash flow planning.

(b) The Flat Rate Scheme (FRS)

The turnover limit, from April 2003, for businesses which want to consider applying to use this scheme is £150,000. The FRS allows VAT to be charged to customers at the rate appropriate to supplies which the business makes, but VAT is accounted for through the VAT Returns at a fixed percentage of all income. The percentage is set by Customs according to the principal activity carried out. Everyday input tax, with certain exceptions, is not claimable under the FRS: this is reflected in the levels at which the various percentages have been fixed. The FRS does not necessarily mean that there is any real saving in how much tax has to be paid. What it does mean is that record-keeping for VAT is cut down, especially when used together with Annual Accounting. If the FRS has attractions for you, you should look carefully at the effect the scheme would have on your own particular business before submitting an application to use it.

Bad debts

Non-payment of bills can cause a lot of concern. Retailers and businesses using cash accounting to work out the VAT on their own supplies do not have to account for output tax until their customers pay them. Similarly input tax may be claimable only when suppliers are paid. Changes have been made in the bad debt VAT rules for those businesses which do not operate on a cash basis. It will now be possible for a business which has charged and accounted for VAT on a supply to a customer to claim back the tax on whatever the unpaid amount may be after six months have elapsed. The other side of the coin is that, for purchases where input tax has been claimed but a supplier's account has not been settled and six months have gone by, the input tax has to be paid back to Customs. Bad debt adjustments, although not shown separately on VAT Returns, have to be recorded in the VAT Account. Listings must be kept to support the entries. Further VAT adjustments are necessary if there are changes in the payments received, or made, later on.

Partial exemption

This is a complex area which occurs when some supplies made by a

VALUE ADDED TAX

business are taxable, whether at a positive or the zero rate, and others are exempt. Strictly, the input tax may only be claimed when it relates to taxable supplies, but this is not always so. A relaxation in the rules allows recovery of all claimable input tax if that which relates to the exempt supplies is less than both £625 per month on average and 50% of the total input tax. The calculations for this have to be done when each VAT Return is completed. An annual adjustment is then carried out to iron out any peaks and troughs which occurred during the year.

Routine compliance checks

Customs have to make sure that businesses are accounting correctly for VAT. When considering the position with your business the VAT Business Centre may invite you to complete a questionnaire and ask for a copy of the most recent annual accounts which have been prepared. Alternatively an officer will arrange to come along and see you. At a visit, the officer will initially want to talk to you and ask questions about your business. This is followed by an examination of your books and records to make sure that you are keeping proper records and correctly dealing with your VAT Returns. The officer will draw your attention to any mistakes which he finds you have made and issue an assessment for any underdeclared or overdeclared tax. Since assessments may span the three years prior to the visit, it is worthwhile reviewing beforehand, as a precautionary measure, the Returns which you have submitted. Misdeclaration penalties and default interest may be imposed if substantial amounts of tax are found to have been underdeclared.

Penalties, surcharges and interest

There are a number of penalties for the registered businesses which are not careful with their VAT records, declarations and payments. Whenever Returns are submitted, the aim should be for the true tax in each and every period to be declared and paid. Getting it right first time is best for everybody's sake. Errors, although they may be innocent, are always possible. If, when you are preparing a Return for a current period, you find you have made mistakes in preceding quarters, you may be able to make an appropriate adjustment without incurring a penalty.

Any errors which, taken altogether, involve an amount of tax less than £2,000 can be adjusted in the Return for a current quarter. However, if the total of any errors exceeds £2,000, spotting where they have been made and what they amount to, and owning up, means that the chance of incurring the misdeclaration penalty may be avoided. Form VAT 652 is available for notifying your VAT Business Centre of errors greater than £2,000. Alternatively, details of any errors of this size may be set out in a letter which should be sent to your VAT Business Centre, together with a payment to correct the overall position. Default interest will normally be charged when assessments for errors are issued.

At the present time the level of the misdeclaration penalty is a flat 15% but whether or not it is imposed depends very much upon the correct amounts of output and input tax which should have been declared for the period.

A further type of penalty may also apply if mistakes are persistently made although, as with other penalties, it may be possible to get it reduced.

Failure to file VAT returns with the VAT Central Unit at Southend-on-Sea and/or pay the proper amount of tax when it is due can lead to the imposition of surcharges. These can range from 2% to 15% if a history of default builds up. Surcharge assessments will, however, seldom be issued unless calculated to exceed £400.

Supplies to/from EU countries

There are special rules for these supplies which, although they may differ from rules covering exports to, and imports from, countries outside the EU, have been designed to help businesses which trade with other member states. Normally, supplies of goods passing between the UK and businesses elsewhere in the EU can be zero-rated provided that the VAT Registration particulars of both parties feature on the invoices. Declarations apart from just the VAT Returns may have to be completed and it is as well to study carefully the appropriate leaflets issued by Customs if your business is likely to be involved with such supplies. How international supplies of services should be dealt with is particularly complicated.

Appeals

If you disagree with an officer's assessment or wish to appeal against a penalty or surcharge, you can ask for the matter to be reconsidered. A review should be carried out by someone at your VAT Business Centre other than the officer who issued the assessment or penalty. Alternatively, an appeal can be lodged for hearing before an independent VAT Tribunal. Lodging an appeal does not prevent you from continuing to discuss or correspond with Customs in the hope that a settlement can be agreed without the need for a Tribunal hearing.

The outcome of Tribunal appeals depends very much upon the reasons why mistakes were made in the first place. Innocence is not normally accepted as an excuse.

Complaints

Standards have been laid down and all Customs officers are expected to abide by them. If you ever feel dissatisfied with the way your business affairs have been handled or that an officer has overstepped the mark and exceeded his authority, you can write to the person who is in overall charge of the VAT Business Centre or directly to the Complaints Unit for the area where your business is situated. The NAS will provide you with the address. Failure to resolve complaints can be followed up by contacting the Adjudicator's Office which is the independent body set up specifically for this purpose.

Customs officers are committed to the same standards as the Inland Revenue — see the Service Commitment reproduced in Chapter 1.

6

THE SELF-EMPLOYED

You cannot simply choose to be taxed as a self-employed person. It is a matter of fact whether you are working on your own account. The concept of self-employment extends to all trades, professions and vocations. You are not self-employed if you are running your business through a company. If you are employed but have some other freelance business activity as well, you will be taxed on these profits as a self-employed person.

Am I self-employed?

The main distinction between self-employed status and working as an employee is the lack of any 'master–servant' relationship. Sometimes it is difficult to distinguish the dividing line between an employment (a contract for service) and self-employment (a contract for services). You are likely to be classified as working on your own account if you:

- Are paid a fee, rather than a fixed hourly rate.
- Have no entitlement to paid holidays or sick leave.
- Do not receive any perks or benefits such as membership of a company pension plan.
- Are responsible for any losses arising out of your services.
- Can dictate how, when and where the work should be undertaken.
- Provide your own tools.

It is not necessary to formalize any business relationship by entering into a formal contract for the supply of your services. Nevertheless, having a contract makes sound business sense because it can deal with matters other than just the tax aspects of the relationship.

Starting up in business

Once you have set yourself up in business you must then come to grips with what you need to do about tax, National Insurance (see Chapter 7) and maybe Value Added Tax (see Chapter 5). I recommend you telephone the Inland Revenue on 08459 15 45 15 and ask for a copy of their booklet 'Starting up in business'. It will help you with what you need to know about keeping proper records as well as dealing with other matters relevant to your new self-employment. The booklet comes with form CWF1 which you need to complete to register for tax and National Insurance. If you fail to notify the Inland Revenue that you have started up in business within three months after the end of the month in which you commenced your self-employment, you will be liable to a fixed penalty of £100.

Records

Under Self-Assessment there is a particular requirement for keeping proper records of all business transactions. The records you should maintain will depend upon the type and size of your business. You are, however, expected to record all of the following:

- sales and other business receipts as they come in, and you should retain the back-up records (for example, invoices, bank statements and paying-in slips to show where the income came from);
- purchases and other expenses for which, wherever possible, you should retain invoices for the goods acquired or costs incurred;
- purchases and sales of assets used in your business;
- amounts taken out of the business for personal use (drawings) and all monies paid into your business from personal funds (capital introduced).

For most businesses it is also good practice to maintain a separate bank account for the business and keep the following books of account, either manually or on computer:

- a cash book which summarizes and analyses all the entries in the bank account;
- a petty cash book to record all small cash transactions.

If you run a larger business you may well need to keep other books of account as well. No matter how large or small your business you would be well advised to keep your accounting records up to date.

You will have to retain your records for five years from the latest date by which your Tax Return has to be filed. For example, your completed Tax Return for the year to 5 April 2003 must be sent back to your tax office by no later than 31 January 2004. It follows that your records for that year must be retained until 31 January 2009.

Accounts

At the end of each financial year all your transactions are brought together into an account of the income and expenditure of the business. Whenever possible a balance sheet should be drawn up showing the assets and liabilities of the business at the year-end.

You can choose the date to which you draw up the accounts of your trade or business each year. For this reason it is unlikely that the first set of accounts will cover a full year's business activities. You can make up your accounts from the date you start in business to the end of:

- A particular month.
- Your first year's trading.

- The calendar year on 31 December.
- The tax year on 5 April.

If your business is a seasonal one it may be a good idea to pick an annual accounting date to coincide with a slack time of the year and when stocks are low. Thereafter you should continue to draw up your accounts to the same date every year, although you can alter this where you can show good reason for a change.

You should also keep in mind that nowadays annual accounts of a business may well be needed for reasons other than tax. For example, your bank manager may want to see your accounts when weighing up an application for a business loan or overdraft facility.

Your accounts should be drawn up to show the profit or loss earned in the financial year. This is not usually the simple difference between the cash received and the cash paid out. For example, if you sell to some of your customers on credit there will inevitably be some unpaid invoices at the end of the financial year. Nevertheless, the amount of these outstanding invoices needs to come into your accounts as income for that period. Equally, where amounts are owing to your suppliers at the year-end these must be brought into the accounts as expenses incurred in the year. If your trade is one where you need to keep a stock of raw materials or finished goods, the value of that stock at the year-end must enter your accounts. It will usually be valued at cost or, in the case of redundant or old stock, at realizable value.

Make sure you include in your accounts all the expenses of running your business. If, for example, you are a married man and your wife helps you by taking telephone messages or acting as your part-time assistant or secretary, pay her a proper wage for these services. What you pay her can count as an expense in your accounts. She can then set off her personal allowance against her wages. If these are less than £4,615 a year there will be no tax or National Insurance to pay on them. There will be some items of expenditure, such as a car used both privately and in your business, when it will be difficult to differentiate precisely between the private and business elements of the expenditure. Where there is this overlap you should agree the proportion which relates to your business with the Inland Revenue. If you do your office work from home you can include as a deduction in your accounts a proportion of your home expenses, such as light, heat and insurance. Remember that if part of your home is used exclusively for business purposes, then should you come to sell your house the profit on sale attributable to that part will not be exempt from Capital Gains Tax.

Illustration

Bob Lancaster is a printer by trade. He operates his business from a rented factory on an industrial estate. His wife keeps his accounts, prepares his VAT returns and acts as part-time secretary.

Bob started up in business in June 1997. He makes up his accounts to 31 October each year. The statement of his business income and expenses for the financial year to 31 October 2002 is as follows:

Bob Lancaster
Printer

Profit and Loss Account for the year ended 31 October 2002

	£	£	£
Sales			267,800
Less: Cost of sales			
Stock of paper and other materials at start of year		3,400	
Purchases during the year		60,700	
		64,100	
Less: Stock of paper and other materials at end of year		3,800	
			60,300
Gross Profit			207,500
Less: Overhead expenses			
Wages and salaries		94,700	
Factory expenses			
Rent and rates	17,840		
Light and heat	4,040		
Cleaning	810		
Insurance	1,310		
Roof repairs	1,880		
		25,880	
Secretarial assistance		4,000	
Printing postage and stationery		920	
Telephone		1,360	
Advertising and promotion		2,900	
Travelling		1,140	
Entertaining		390	
Accountancy		1,850	
Legal Fees – new lease		730	
Car expenses			
Road Fund Licence and Insurance	880		
Petrol and oil	1,270		
Repairs and servicing	410		
	2,560		
Business proportion	75%	1,920	

STANDARD ACCOUNTING INFORMATION

Use of home as office	($1/7$ × 1,610)	230	
Home telephone	(25%)	360	
Bank interest and charges		4,280	
Provision for bad debts	(10% × 21,300)	2,130	
Miscellaneous expenses		710	
			143,500
Profit for the year			**£64,000**

Standard accounting information

If at any time during the 2002/03 tax year you were in business then you will need to fill in the self-employment pages of your Tax Return for that year. For those in business with a turnover of more than £15,000 there is now a set format, as part of the self-employment pages of the Return, for reporting the annual income and expenses of your business. If accounts are not presented in the required format the Return will not be accepted as complete.

Illustration

When Bob Lancaster, the printer, comes to complete the self-employment pages of his Tax Return for the year ended 5 April 2003 he will fill in the section on business income and expenses for his financial year to 31 October 2002 as follows:

	£	£
Sales/business income (excluding VAT)		267,800
Less: Cost of sales	60,300	
Other direct costs	–	
		60,300
Gross profit		207,500
Other income/profits		–
		207,500
Less: Expenses		
Employee costs	98,700	
Premises costs	24,230	
Repairs	1,880	
General administrative expenses	2,640	
Motor expenses	1,920	
Travel and subsistence	1,140	
Advertising, promotion and entertainment	3,290	
Legal and professional costs	2,580	

Bad debts	2,130	
Interest	4,280	
Other finance charges	–	
Depreciation and loss/(profit) on sale	–	
Other expenses	710	
Total expenses		143,500
Net profit		£64,000

Notes:–

(1) Employee costs are:

	£
Wages and salaries	94,700
Wife's salary	4,000
	£98,700

(2) Premises costs are:

Factory – rent and rates	17,840
– light and heat	4,040
– insurance	1,310
– cleaning	810
Use of home as office	230
	£24,230

(3) General administrative expenses are:

Printing postage and stationery	920
Telephone (factory and home)	1,720
	2,640

(4) Legal and professional costs are:

Accountancy	1,850
Legal fees	730
	£2,580

In order to minimize the risk of an Inland Revenue enquiry into your business accounts and Tax Return, it is important that the analysis of your business expenses over the various headings in the standardized accounting format follows a consistent pattern from year to year.

If the total annual turnover of your business is below £15,000 you can fill in the special, shortened income and expenses section in the self-employment pages of the Return. This comprises a three-line statement of:

- turnover and other business receipts;
- business expenses allowable for tax;
- resulting profit or loss.

You should, of course, still keep proper business accounts and records in order that you can draw up the annual three-line statement accurately.

Adjustment of profits

It does not follow that the profit shown by your business accounts is the same as the one on which you pay tax. This is because some items of expenditure are specifically not deductible in computing your taxable business profits. Types of expenditure which come into this category are business entertainment, non-business charitable donations, general provisions and reserves, professional costs related to capital expenditure, and the cost of items of a capital, as opposed to revenue, nature.

Illustration

Although Bob Lancaster's accounts for his financial year to 31 October 2002 show a profit of £64,000, his taxable profits are £67,250, as follows:

	£	£
Profit as per accounts		64,000
Add Disallowable expenses:		
General provision for bad debts	2,130	
Entertainment	390	
Legal fees for new lease	730	
		3,250
Profit as adjusted for tax purposes		£67,250

The current-year basis of taxation

Under the current-year basis of taxation, self-employed individuals are taxed on the profits made in the tax year. The profits shown by annual accounts drawn up to a date other than the end of the tax year – 'the basis period' – are regarded as those of the year to 5 April.

Illustration

The tax-adjusted profit of £67,250 of Bob Lancaster's printing business for the year to 31 October 2002 will be taxed in 2002/03.

For the first year of business the taxable profits will be limited to those arising in the period from commencement to 5 April. On cessation the profits for the final tax year will be those arising in the period from the end of the basis period taxed in the previous tax year.

Under these rules it is possible that some periods of account will feature for more than one tax year. However, over the lifetime of a business it is intended that the profits should be taxed in full, once and once only. Accordingly, any profits which are taxed more than once will be eligible for a special relief. Known as overlap relief, it will be given either when a business ceases or for any earlier tax year for which the basis period is longer than 12 months.

Illustration

James Gray started his business on 1 September 2002. His annual accounting date is 31 August. He makes the following profits:

Year to 31.08.2003	£15,900
Year to 31.08.2004	£19,200

The taxable profits for the first three tax years are:

Tax Year	Basis Period	Taxable Profit
		£
2002/03	01.09.2002 to 05.04.2003	9,275
2003/04	Year to 31.08.2003	15,900
2004/05	Year to 31.08.2004	19,200

The business closes down on 30 April 2009. The taxable profit in the final period from 1 September 2008 to 30 April 2009 amounts to £12,000. The final tax year is 2009/10 when James will be taxable on:

		£
Taxable profit in final period		12,000
Less: Overlap	01.09.2002 to 05.04.2003	9,275
Net taxable amount		£2,725

Special rules apply when a business changes its accounting date. Apart from the first and last years of business the system aims to tax the profits of a 12-month period in each tax year.

Illustration

Sheila Windows commenced her business on 1 October 2002. She draws up her first accounts to 30 September 2003 which disclose a profit of £19,000. She then changes her accounting date to 31 December 2004. The accounts for the 15-month period show a taxable profit of £15,000. Her basis periods and taxable profits for the opening years of her business are:

Tax Year	Basis Period	Taxable Profit £
2002/03	01.10.2002 to 05.04.2003	9,500
2003/04	Year to 30.09.2003	19,000

The overlap period is from 01.10.2002 to 05.04.2003:

2004/05	01.10.2003 to 31.12.2004 (15 months)	15,000
Less: Overlap	01.10.2002 to 31.12.2002	4,750
Net taxable amount		£10,250

The overlap period was one of six months. As the accounting period from 1 October 2003 to 31 December 2004 is 15 months, the overlap relief is three months. The amount deducted from the taxable profits for 2004/05 is ½ of the original overlap profit. A further three months of overlap relief is then available either when the business ceases or for any subsequent tax year when the basis period is longer than 12 months.

Post-cessation expenses

Tax relief is allowed on specific types of expense incurred after a business has ceased. Relief is available for payments made within seven years of the permanent discontinuance of the business. The types of expense which qualify for this form of relief are those closely related to the trading or professional activities while they were carried on. Included, for example, is relief for debts which subsequently proved to be irrecoverable.

The relief is given by setting the payments made against income for the same tax year. Any excess can be treated as a capital loss of the same year only. Any unrelieved post-cessation expenses cannot be carried back or forward against either income or capital gains.

Capital allowances

Although you cannot deduct expenditure on items of a capital nature directly from your business profits, you do receive what are known as capital allowances on the expenditure.

Amounts spent by small and medium-sized businesses (your business is almost certain to qualify) attract the following rates of allowance in the first year:

- 40% for expenditure on plant and machinery, but not motor cars;
- 100% where the investment is in information and communications technology. This enhanced rate of first year allowance applies to expenditure on computers, software and internet-enabled mobile phones and similar devices incurred in the three years from 1 April 2000.
- 100% for purchases of new low-emission cars for use by you or your employees in your business. To qualify for this relief, a car must be first registered on or after 17 April 2002 and either emit not more than 120 gm/km CO_2 or be electrically propelled.
- 25% for other motor cars. For cars costing more than £12,000 there is a maximum allowance of £3,000.

In subsequent years, the balance of expenditure is written down on the reducing-balance basis at the rate of 25% p.a. For cars the maximum writing-down allowance is restricted to £3,000 in a year.

A separate 'pool' of expenditure must be maintained for each of the following different categories:

- plant and equipment, including motor vans, lorries and cars costing up to £12,000;
- each car bought for over £12,000;
- each asset used for both personal and business use;
- each asset with a short life expectancy.

Where an asset on which capital allowances have been given is sold, the proceeds of sale must come into the computation of capital allowances. This can sometimes lead to a further allowance where an asset is sold for less than its written-down value for tax purposes. Alternatively, if it fetches an amount greater than its written-down value this can often mean that part of the allowances already given needs to be withdrawn. These adjustments are respectively referred to as balancing allowances and balancing charges.

Illustration
In his accounting year to 31 October 2002, our printer, Bob Lancaster, traded in his old car for £2,000 and bought a new car for £11,600. In June of the year he also spent £6,000 on a binding machine. His claim to capital

allowances for 2002/03, based on his capital expenditure in the year to 31 October 2002, is:

	Pool £	Car with Private Use £
Written-down values brought forward from 2001/02	3,260	2,640
Sale proceeds of car		2,000
Balancing allowance		640
Additions in the year:		
Binding machine	6,000	
New car		11,600
	9,260	
Allowances due:		
First year – 40% 2,400		
Writing down – 25% 815	3,215	2,900
Carried forward to 2003/04	£6,045	£8,700
Summary of allowances:		
First year		2,400
Writing down		3,715
Balancing		640
		6,755
Less: 25% private use of car		885
2002/03 Capital allowances		£5,870

Capital allowances are treated as a trading expense of your business. Any balancing charges are added to your profit as a trading receipt. It follows that the chargeable period for the purposes of calculating your capital allowances is the same as that for which you draw up your accounts. This means that the amount of writing-down allowances to which you are entitled is determined by reference to the length of the period of account. Thus, if you draw up accounts for an eight-month period, $8/_{12}$ of the writing-down allowances can be set against taxable profits for that period. Similarly, if a period of account extends to 15 months the tax deductible allowances are equivalent to $15/_{12}$ of the writing-down allowances. In the event that a period of account exceeds 18 months it will be divided into one of 12 months and the balancing period with a restricted writing-down allowance.

Under Self-Assessment there is a section in the self-employment pages of your Tax Return for you to summarize your claim to capital allowances.

Losses
Most businesses cannot escape going through a bad spell at some stage in their existence. Where the results of your business for the year show a loss you will be able to claim tax relief on the loss as increased by any claim to capital allowances which count as trading expenses. You can elect to set a trading loss against other income for the same tax year, or the preceding year. You cannot claim relief for only part of a loss.

Illustration
Martin Peters has been in business for many years. He makes up his accounts to 30 November each year. He makes a loss in the year ended 30 November 2003 which can be claimed against his other income in 2003/04 and/or carried back and relieved against his total income in 2002/03.

Any unrelieved loss of your business must then be carried forward to be set against the profits from the same business in later years.

Otherwise you can claim to offset a trading loss against capital gains as follows:
- The claim is for relief on the amount of the trading loss which cannot be set against your other income in the year or on which tax relief has already been allowed in some other way.

- The maximum loss eligible for relief against capital gains is equivalent to the amount of your gains chargeable to Capital Gains Tax before taper relief is applied.

- It is not possible to make a partial claim.

- It is possible that personal allowances may be wasted as well as the annual exemption for Capital Gains Tax (see Chapter 12).

There is an alternative form of loss relief available for new businesses where:
- Losses incurred during the first four years of assessment are allowed to be set against your income in the three years prior to that in which the loss arises.
- Relief is first of all given against your income for the earliest year. For example, if you started out in business during 2002/03 and incurred a loss in the first period of trading, the proportion attributable to the tax year 2002/03 can be set off against your income in 1999/2000, 2000/01 and 2001/02, starting with 1999/2000.

THE ENTERPRISE ALLOWANCE

Frequently it is necessary to incur expenditure on a new business venture before it starts to trade. Any such expenditure incurred within seven years prior to the commencement of trade is treated as a separate loss sustained in the tax year in which trading began.

There is also a special form of loss relief for those businesses which incur a loss in their final period of trading. As the business has ceased there cannot be any future profits against which the loss might be relieved. Therefore, you are allowed to set a loss arising in the last 12 months of trading against the profits from the same business in the final tax year as well as the three preceding years, beginning with the profits of the last year and working backwards.

Illustration

Ralph Collins retires from business on 30 November 2003. Apart from the final eight months when he loses £21,000 his business had always been successful. His recent taxable profits had been as follows:

Accounting Year		Taxable Profits £	Year of Charge
Year ended 31 March	2000	12,000	1999/2000
Year " " "	2001	15,000	2000/01
Year " " "	2002	6,000	2001/02
Year " " "	2003	8,000	2002/03

The terminal loss can be set off as follows:

2002/03	8,000	leaving nil taxable profits
2001/02	6,000	leaving nil taxable profits
2000/01	7,000	reducing the taxable profits to £8,000
	£21,000	

The Enterprise Allowance

The Enterprise Allowance is a weekly payment for one year to individuals leaving the unemployment register to set up in business. The allowance is not included in the takings of the recipient's business, although it is chargeable to Income Tax.

Taking on an employee

If you are thinking of taking on an assistant or an extra pair of hands for the first time, you should inform your tax office dealing with your business. They will immediately send the information to the right tax office since it is likely to be a different office to that dealing with your business. You should then receive a New Employer's Starter Pack containing all the instructions, tables and forms you will need.

As an employer you are responsible for:

- Working out the deductions for Income Tax (PAYE) and National Insurance Contributions from the salary or wage of your employees each pay day, whether this be weekly or monthly.

- Paying over the deductions to the Collector of Taxes each month. These payments can be made every quarter where your average monthly payments of tax and National Insurance Contributions are less than £1,500.

- Letting your tax office know every year how much each employee has earned and the deductions you have made for Income Tax and National Insurance Contributions. All the deductions should reconcile to the total of the amounts paid over to the Collector of Taxes. You must also give details of any benefits paid or provided.

- Giving your employees certificates showing their earnings for the tax year, deductions for Income Tax and National Insurance Contributions and the value of any benefits provided.

Special situations

In the space available it has only been possible for me to paint a general picture of the way in which business profits are taxed. If you are a Lloyd's underwriter, a farmer, a writer or a subcontractor in the construction industry you should be aware that there are special rules which apply in calculating the tax on the profits from your trade or profession.
In these and other situations it is advisable to seek professional assistance.

The letting of holiday accommodation in the UK is treated as a trade. The accommodation has to be furnished residential property which is available for renting by the public as holiday accommodation for at least 140 days during each tax year. It must actually be let for a minimum of 70 days. There are other requirements which also need to be satisfied. Capital gains on disposals of holiday accommodation falling within these rules qualify for the replacement and retirement reliefs which apply to business assets (see Chapter 12).

7

NATIONAL INSURANCE CONTRIBUTIONS, STATE SOCIAL SECURITY AND INSURED BENEFITS

Whether you are employed or self-employed, you will have to pay National Insurance Contributions, as well as Income Tax, by reference to your earnings or business profits. In turn, the payment of sufficient National Insurance Contributions makes you eligible to claim those Social Security benefits which are based on your contribution history. Many benefits, however, such as those payable to the Disabled, do not depend upon the payment of contributions.

National Insurance Contributions

There are four different types of contribution which are payable:

- Class 1 by employees;
- Class 2 by the self-employed;
- Class 3 which is voluntary;
- Class 4 by the self-employed, based on profits.

You will not be liable for contributions once you have retired and passed normal retirement age, which is 60 for a woman and 65 for a man, even if you carry on working for someone else or in your own business.

For National Insurance the earnings of employees on which Class 1 contributions are calculated include:

- a salary or wage – before deduction for pension contributions;
- overtime, bonuses and commission;
- holiday pay;
- statutory sick and maternity pay.

However, no contributions are payable by employees on benefits-in-kind.

Your contributions are usually worked out as a percentage of your weekly or monthly salary or wage, subject to lower and upper earnings limits. If you choose to have a break when moving jobs, or there is a period when you are unemployed, this has no effect on the contributions you will have to pay when you go back to work.

There are special rules for company directors. The contributions due from a company director are worked out on the basis that each tax year is an earnings period even if the director is paid monthly or leaves during the year.

If you have more than one employment you are liable for contributions on your earnings from all your employers. Nevertheless there is an overall annual maximum limit of contributions payable by employees. Where the total amount of deductions for your National Insurance Contributions exceeds this annual limit then you should apply for a refund of the overpayment. Alternatively you can apply for deferment where you can envisage that the contributions which will be taken off your earnings from two or more employments are such that the total deductions will exceed the maximum annual limit. To apply for deferment you will need to complete a form CF379 before the beginning of the tax year when you want to defer the payment of contributions. The Contributions Office of the Inland Revenue will then instruct one or other of your employers not to withhold contributions from your earnings. After the end of the tax year your overall contribution history for that year is reviewed. If, for some reason or another, insufficient contributions have been collected on the earnings from all employments then the Contributions Office will send you a calculation and demand for the balance due.

There are two rates of National Insurance Contributions payable by the self-employed. Class 2 is a weekly flat rate. You can pay by either direct debit every month or by quarterly bill every 13 weeks. If your earnings are below a specified annual limit you can be exempted from paying these contributions. You should apply in advance for small-earnings exception. Class 4 contributions are based on a percentage of your taxable business profits, after capital allowances, but before relief for pension contributions. These are accounted for through the tax system along with the annual tax liability on your profits as a self-employed taxpayer.

In certain circumstances, for example where you are also in employment and paying Class 1 contributions, you can apply to defer payment of both Class 2 and Class 4 contributions.

The payment of Class 3 contributions is voluntary. An individual who is neither employed nor in self-employment can pay Class 3 contributions in order to preserve entitlement to the state pension on retirement.

The rates of National Insurance Contributions for 2002/03 are in Table 4 at the end of the book. Your nearest Inland Revenue (National Insurance Contributions) office will supply you with leaflets and forms relating to National Insurance contributions. Table 5 is a list of those leaflets with the widest application.

State Retirement Pensions

There are three types of state retirement pension:

- the basic retirement (or old person's) pension;
- a state earnings-related pension (SERPS);
- a graduated pension.

STATE RETIREMENT PENSIONS

State retirement pensions are payable to men who have reached age 65 and to women aged 60, subject, of course, to their contribution history. The contribution requirements which you must meet before you are entitled to the basic state pension are:

- The payment of Class 1, 2 or 3 National Insurance Contributions in any one tax year since 6 April 1975 such as to make that year a qualifying year. This is one in which you have received qualifying earnings equivalent to at least 52 times the lower weekly earnings limit for National Insurance purposes for that year. Alternatively, you must actually have paid 50 flat-rate contributions at any time before 6 April 1975.

- The establishment of qualifying years for around 90% of your working life before you can receive the full basic pension. You need nine or ten qualifying years to get the minimum – 25% – basic pension payable.

As the name implies, the state earnings-related pension scheme (SERPS) is dependent on your earnings. You can get this additional pension if in any tax year since April 1978 you have paid the standard rate of Class 1 National Insurance Contributions on earnings between the lower and upper earnings limits. Furthermore, each Class 2 Contribution paid by the self-employed counts as one week's earnings at the lower earnings limit applying in that year.

As well as being entitled to the basic and additional pensions, certain individuals will be entitled to a pension under the graduated scheme. This was in operation between April 1961 and April 1975.

In addition to the basic pension a man may receive extra pension for:

- a wife;

- dependent children;

- a woman looking after his children.

A married woman may benefit from a retirement pension in one or other of three distinct ways:

- on her own contribution record;

- based on her husband's contribution if she is over 60 and retired so long as her husband is receiving a basic retirement pension;

- as a wife dependent on her husband. He is then entitled to an increase in his pension.

The retirement pension payable to a widow will depend on whether she was widowed before the normal retirement age of 60 or was widowed afterwards.

Social Security Benefits

It is the Department for Work and Pensions (DWP) which is responsible for administering all aspects of the social security system. There are local DWP offices throughout the country. The framework of the social security system is now so substantial, and the range of benefits so wide and varied, it is only possible for me to give a brief summary of the main benefits.

Many benefits are only payable to individuals who have an established history of paying National Insurance Contributions. The type of benefit you can then claim depends on the nature of contributions paid as follows:

Type of Benefit	Class 1 (Employed)	Class 2 (Self-Employed)	Class 3 (Voluntary)
Retirement Pension			
– basic	Yes	Yes	Yes
– additional	Yes	No	No
– widow's	Yes	Yes	Yes
Bereavement allowance	Yes	Yes	Yes
Bereavement payment	Yes	Yes	Yes
Widowed parent's allowance	Yes	Yes	Yes
Widow's Payment	Yes	Yes	Yes
Incapacity benefit	Yes	Yes	No
Jobseeker's allowance	Yes	No	No
Statutory Sick and Maternity Pay	Yes	No	No

Other benefits do not depend upon the payment of contributions. Equally some benefits paid to you by the state are taxable, others are tax free.

To be able to claim either statutory sick or maternity pay you must be earning enough to pay Class 1 National Insurance Contributions. A woman will qualify for statutory maternity pay if she has been working for the same employer continuously for 26 weeks up to, and including, the 15th week before her baby is due. She must provide evidence of being pregnant and give her employer sufficient notice of leaving work. The benefit is payable for 18 weeks beginning not earlier than the 11th week before the baby is due although the woman can actually select the time over which she will be absent from work.

Statutory sick pay is a flat-rate cash payment made to employees by their employer. To be eligible to claim you must be both incapable of work and not actually do any work at all on the day in question. It is not payable for the first three agreed qualifying days in any period when you are too unwell to work. In any period of sickness you have a maximum entitlement to 28 weeks of statutory sick pay.

SOCIAL SECURITY BENEFITS

Incapacity benefit is a benefit for individuals under state pension age, provided they have paid a qualifying amount of National Insurance Contributions, who are unable to work because of illness or disability. Employees will normally get statutory sick pay for the first 28 weeks of sickness before moving on to incapacity benefit at the short-term higher rate. There are three different rates of benefit and additional supplements which may be paid. Incapacity benefit is not means-tested, but it is taxable. Any tax due will be deducted directly from the benefit paid to claimants who do not have another source of income already subject to PAYE. Where claimants do have another source of income on which PAYE is applied – such as an occupational pension from a former employer – any tax due on the benefit will be collected by adjusting the tax code applied to the other income and deducting tax from that other income.

In order to claim the jobseeker's allowance an individual needs to satisfy a number of conditions. The main features of the jobseeker's allowance, which is taxable, are that:

- entitlement is based on either a satisfactory contribution record or a means-tested low income;

- it is a weekly benefit with supplements for age and other personal circumstances;

- it is payable to unemployed individuals between the ages of 18 and state pensionable age. A claimant must sign a jobseeker's agreement which sets out the steps he or she intends to take towards full-time employment.

An individual is disqualified from receiving benefit if he or she fails to honour the obligations of the jobseeker's agreement, or refuses to follow either recommendations or directions of the employment advisor.

Other benefits include:

- income support, which is a non-contributory weekly benefit paid to individuals who do not have sufficient money to live on. The needs of each claimant are assessed depending on their circumstances. However, claimants with savings and capital over £8,000 do not qualify for income support.

- child benefit, which is not means tested and is payable to individuals bringing up children. For couples who are married it is the wife who should make the claim. The benefit is payable for all children under 16 years old. Children over age 15, but under 19, still qualify providing they are still in full-time education which includes courses at school or college up to 'A' Level. Child benefit is not payable for children studying beyond this level – for example for a university degree.

- benefits for employees who suffer personal injury from an accident arising out of their employment. The injury can result in either physical or mental impairment.
- benefits for the disabled such as the attendance and invalid care allowances. The attendance allowance is targeted at individuals who are seriously disabled, mentally or physically, and who need a lot of care and attention. On the other hand the invalid care allowance is payable to those individuals who are unable to work because they have to look after a relative who is either sick or disabled.

All the social security benefits, distinguishing between those which are taxable and non-taxable, are listed in Table 6 at the end of the book. The rates of the main taxable social security benefits for 2002/03 are in Table 7.

Insured benefits
Benefits paid under insurance policies which provide against financial loss caused by unemployment, accident, sickness disability or infirmity are not taxable. The different types of insurance policy with tax-free benefits are:
- mortgage payment protection insurance: these provide income to meet mortgage commitments in the event of accident, sickness, disability or unemployment;
- permanent health insurance: these provide continuing income in the event of accident, sickness or disability;
- creditor insurance: these provide benefits to meet existing obligations and commitments, such as loans and domestic utility bills;
- certain kinds of long-term care insurance: that is those which provide benefits to meet the cost of the provision of care in the event of accident, sickness, disability or infirmity but only where policies are taken out before the need for care becomes apparent.

8

PERSONAL PENSIONS

Wherever possible I imagine you will want to avoid a drop in your living standards when you come to retire and will be looking to your pension plan to replace, at the very least, some part of your previous earnings or business profits. To give you the best possible opportunity of building up a worthwhile pension, to supplement your entitlement to the State Pension, you should start contributing to an appropriate plan as soon as you can reasonably afford to do so.

Many employers, particularly large organizations, have long-established Company Pension Schemes and have been offering employees membership of their schemes for a considerable number of years. If you are employed by such an organization you should satisfy the requirements to join their pension scheme. Some employers do not require their employees to make any contributions towards their benefits on retirement. In other cases employees must contribute a percentage of their annual salary in addition to the amount that their employer pays into their schemes each year.

Employers with 5 or more employees (including directors) must provide their employees with access to a designated Stakeholder Pension Scheme, or offer a satisfactory alternative. Although such employers must offer a Stakeholder Pension Scheme there is no requirement that they need contribute nor are employees bound to join the scheme.

If your employer has not set up his own scheme for his employees or you are self-employed you will need to make your own personal pension arrangements.

Eligible individuals
To be eligible to take out a personal pension plan you must be resident and ordinarily resident in the UK for at least part of a tax year. You can do so if:

- you are self-employed;

- you are in employment. You can choose to opt out of your employer's own company scheme and take out a personal pension plan instead. Your employer can make contributions into your personal pension plan in addition to the amount of premiums you pay into the plan;

- you opt out of the state earnings-related pension scheme (SERPS). The Department of Work and Pensions will then pay the difference between the full and reduced rates of National Insurance Contributions into your personal pension scheme. Opting out of SERPS does not affect your entitlement to the basic State Pension.

- you are neither employed nor self-employed. In such circumstances the maximum contribution limit is £3,600 (gross) per annum.

Benefits on retirement

When you start making regular monthly or annual contributions into a personal pension plan do remember you cannot benefit from the funds building up in your plan until you come to retire and draw your pension. Throughout this period your contributions will be invested in a tax-free fund. As we will see later on in this chapter you will also receive tax relief on your premiums. You benefit from a further tax concession on retirement when 25% of the value of the fund built up in your personal pension plan can be paid to you as a tax-free lump sum. The remainder of your fund is used to provide a pension which will be payable throughout the rest of your life. You can even arrange for this to be paid for a minimum guaranteed period, usually five years, should you die within this period. It is also possible to provide for a dependant's pension if you die before your spouse. As we will see in Chapter 10 the pension you eventually come to draw from your scheme is taxable.

The tax-free lump sum and pension can be taken at any time between the ages of 50 and 75. You do not actually need to retire before taking your pension. The Inland Revenue has approved earlier retirement ages of 30, 35, 40 or 45 for some professions and occupations, particularly in professional sport; for example, footballers can retire at age 35 and take maximum benefits. Those benefits within your plan which were purchased through opting out of SERPS cannot be drawn until you reach normal state retirement age.

If unfortunately you die before retirement a lump sum, depending on the terms of your particular plan, will probably be refundable. This can be paid out to beneficiaries nominated by you during your lifetime or, alternatively, to your executors. Any lump sum payable is free of tax.

Deferred annuities

Holders of personal pension plans can defer, if they wish, the purchase of their annuity up to age 75. In the meantime, during the deferral period, they can make income withdrawals taxable under PAYE in the same way as annuities. There is a set formula for working out the maximum amount of income withdrawal, which must be reviewed every three years.

During the period of deferral, the pension fund remains tax free and protected from Inheritance Tax. However, no further contributions can then be made into the plan.

Should the personal pension plan holder die after benefits have been taken from the plan, but before the annuity has been purchased, a surviving spouse or dependant has three options:

- for the time being to continue making income withdrawals. The annuity can be purchased either on the deceased's 75th birthday or his or her own 75th birthday, whichever is the earlier;
- to purchase an annuity immediately;
- to take the fund in cash, when there will be a special 35% tax charge on the value of the fund.

Tax relief on premiums

All contributions into personal pension plans are paid after deduction of tax at the basic rate – currently 22%. Should you be liable to tax at the higher rate of 40%, and be in employment, you will need to tell your tax office about your personal pension plan so that the extra tax relief on your premiums over and above that due at the basic rate can be allowed in your code number. Other taxpayers can claim their higher rate tax relief as part of their annual self-assessment.

Annual premiums in excess of £3,600 gross can only be paid based on earnings. For:

- employees, earnings include the annual amount of taxable benefits-in-kind.
- the self-employed, earnings are the annual taxable business profits as reduced by capital allowances and any losses.

The most you can contribute each year is expressed as a percentage of your earnings and depends on your age. Furthermore, there is a maximum earnings limit on which the percentage limit can be calculated. For 2002/03 this is £97,200. It increases each year in line with the movement in the Retail Prices Index. The contribution limits are as follows:

Age at Start of Tax Year	Percentage Limit of Earnings %
Under 36	17½
36–45	20
46–50	25
51–55	30
56–60	35
Over 60	40

The maximum pension contributions payable can be based on the appropriate percentage of the higher of an individual's net relevant earnings for:

- that tax year, or
- in any of the five preceding tax years.

This rule will be of particular help for those in self-employment whose profits often fluctuate from one year to the next.

Up to 10% of your annual premiums can be paid into a policy providing for the payment of a lump sum to your dependants in the event of your death before the age of 75.

Premiums paid in the year can either be deducted from your taxable income in the year of payment, or alternatively you can elect for them to be treated as if paid in the preceding year providing you do not exceed the contribution limit for the earlier year. Premiums carried back to the previous tax year must be paid before 31 January following the end of the tax year. The election to carry back the tax relief to the previous year must be made on or before the date of payment of the premiums.

Retirement annuities

Personal pension schemes, in one form or another, have been around since the beginning of July 1988. Up to that date the self-employed and employees who were not members of their employer's own pension schemes could take out retirement annuities. No new retirement annuities may now be taken out although you can continue to pay regular and single premiums into existing contracts. Retirement annuities differ from personal pension plans in a number of ways:

- employers are not allowed to make contributions into them;
- although there is no maximum earnings limit on which premiums may be paid, the contribution limits are not so generous:

Age at Start of Tax Year	Percentage Limit of Earnings %
Under 51	17½
51–55	20
56–60	22½
Over 60	27½

- you cannot draw your benefits before age 60. It is possible to transfer the benefits under a retirement annuity to a personal pension in order to draw down the tax-free lump sum and pension before age 60;

- if you are in employment you cannot pay your premiums after the deduction at source of tax at the basic rate;
- the method of calculating the maximum amount of the tax-free lump sum on retirement is more generous.
- where you do not pay premiums up to the maximum permissible amount in any year the shortfall can be carried forward for up to six years. Relief outstanding for earlier years is used up before that still available for later years.

Illustration

Peter Wong has been in business for many years. Since 1998/99 Peter has not been making the maximum contributions into his retirement annuity contract as follows:

Tax Year	Premiums Paid £	Maximum Permissible £	Shortfall £
1998/99	1,300	2,400	1,100
1999/2000	1,400	1,800	400
2000/01	1,000	2,000	1,000
2001/02	1,500	2,300	800

During 2002/03 Peter paid premiums of £5,000; the maximum permissible premium limit for the year was only £2,000. Nevertheless relief will be given for £5,000, as follows:

	£	£
Premium limit for 2002/03		2,000
Unused relief:		
1998/99	1,100	
1999/2000	400	
2000/01	1,000	
2001/02 (part)	500	
		3,000
2002/03 Pension premium relief		£5,000

Personal pension planning

If you are still contributing into a retirement annuity you will often have to decide between continuing with this policy or instead opting to take out a personal pension plan. Where your salary or profits fall short of the earnings 'cap' of £97,200 you should consider contributing as much as you can into an existing retirement annuity as well as taking advantage of the higher contribution limits for personal pensions.

Illustration

John Wallace aged 44 earns £54,000 per annum. He has an existing retirement annuity and pays premiums of £5,200 each year.

John's maximum contribution limits are:

(1) Into his retirement annuity – £9,450 (17½% × £54,000)

(2) Into a personal pension – £10,800 (20% × £54,000)

John can pay either:

(a) A further £4,250 into his retirement annuity and contribute £1,350 into a personal pension, or

(b) A premium of £5,600 into a personal pension.

If you earn more than the amounts in the following table you should consider paying the maximum premiums into your retirement annuity.

Age at 6 April 2002	Earnings £
Under 36	97,200
36–45	111,085
46–50	138,857
51–55	145,800
56–60	151,200
Over 60	141,382

Illustration

Veronica Adams aged 48 earns £150,000 per annum. She has an existing retirement annuity and contributes £12,000 each year.

Veronica's maximum contribution limits are:

(1) Into her retirement annuity – £26,250 (17½% × £150,000)

(2) Into a personal pension – £24,300 (25% × £97,200)

Veronica can either contribute:

(a) A further £14,250 into her retirement annuity, or

(b) A premium into a personal pension plan. If she chooses to do so the total additional contributions she can make into the new personal pension and her existing retirement annuity between them are £12,300.

If your earnings are below the amounts in the above table you should again contribute the maximum amount into your existing retirement annuity and top this up by paying a further premium into a personal pension plan.

Illustration

Alan Potter aged 57 earns £110,000 per annum. He has a retirement annuity and pays premiums of £13,000 annually.

Alan's maximum contribution limits are:

(1) Into his retirement annuity – £24,750 (22½% x £110,000)

(2) Into a personal pension – £34,020 (35% x £97,200)

Alan can either contribute:

(a) A further £11,750 into his retirement annuity and pay a personal pension premium of £9,270, or

(b) An amount of £21,020 into a personal pension.

9

INVESTMENT INCOME

Most of you will at some time or other need to look into the various types of investment on offer. Perhaps you will be looking to find a suitable home for regular savings or to invest a more substantial amount such as an inheritance or a lump sum on retirement. Investment or unearned income is that which does not depend on your active involvement or physical effort in some business or trade. Bank or building society interest, dividends on shares or unit trust holdings, rents, income from a trust and interest on government stocks are all investment income.

Tax-free income

The most widely known investments where the return is free of both Income Tax and Capital Gains Tax are some of those available from the Department of National Savings. They are:

- Fixed-Interest and Index-linked Savings Certificates;

- Premium Bond prizes;

- first £70 of annual interest on a National Savings Bank Ordinary Account.

    Also tax free is:

- interest on your TESSA, provided you do not touch the capital;

- income from your PEP and ISA investments;

- dividends you receive on shares you own in Venture Capital Trusts.

    Apart from interest on any National Savings Bank account, no details of these need to be shown on your annual Income Tax Return.

Rental income

The letting of property, including isolated or casual lettings, is treated as a business for tax purposes. This applies to a flat, house, shop or any other property which you let out to tenants. Most of the rules currently in force for working out the taxable profits from a trade or profession also apply in calculating your annual profits from let property. All income from property situated in the United Kingdom is pooled together, regardless of the type of lease. It does not matter whether the property is furnished or unfurnished. Losses from your business of renting out property can be carried forward to be set against future profits of your income from the property business.

Apart from expenditure of a capital nature, such as that on structural alterations or improvements, the general running costs of a property can be set against rental income. Allowable expenses include:

- amounts spent on letting out the property including estate agents' fees, advertising expenses and the costs of drawing up an inventory;

- interest relating to your property letting business. It matters not whether the interest is payable on a loan or overdraft;

- rent collection costs;

- maintenance, repairs and redecorations;

- premiums on buildings and contents insurance policies;

- rent and water rates;

- Council Tax which you pay for your tenants;

- all other expenses of managing the property such as stationery, postage, etc.;

- your share of expenditure on the common parts of the let property.

Illustration

	£	£
Rent receivable from let property		18,000
Less: Expenses		
Rent collection costs	2,115	
Council Tax	620	
Water rates	210	
Building insurance premium	290	
Roof repairs	752	
Garden maintenance	340	
		4,327
2002/03 net rental income		£13,673

If your gross rental income before expenses is less than £15,000 in the year, you do not need to list the expenses separately. The total expenses can be entered on your Return as one amount.

Where you are renting out property which is unfurnished, you can claim capital allowances on the cost of fixtures, fittings and equipment incurred on the let property.

If you are letting a furnished property you can claim an additional deduction to cover the cost of wear and tear to furnishings and fittings. This can be what you actually spend on renewing fixtures and fittings. Alternatively you can claim a fixed allowance of 10% of the rent less amounts paid out on water rates and Council Tax. If the property in the preceding illustration is let furnished this allowance would be £1,144 as follows:

Illustration

	£
Rent receivable	18,000
Less: Water rates and Council Tax	830
	£17,170
Wear and tear allowance: 10%	£1,717

The rules dealing with the taxation of premiums on leases are more complicated and outside the scope of this book.

Rent-a-Room

Income from the furnished letting of spare rooms in your home is tax-free providing the annual gross rents do not exceed £4,250 per annum. The space you let out must be in your only or main home. This can be a house, flat, caravan or even a houseboat. You can choose to opt out of the special form of relief. You will then be taxed under the normal rules dealing with income from furnished lettings. If, for example, there was a loss on the letting which could be set against other income then it would pay you to make the opt-out election.

Where your annual gross rents are more than £4,250 then you can pay tax on the excess gross rents, without any relief for expenses, or under the rules for taxing furnished lettings income.

Illustration

Theresa Stevens, who is a basic rate taxpayer, lets a room in her house for £4,800 per annum.

The expenses which can be set against the income total £1,400. Under the Rent-a-Room relief her Income Tax liability is £121.00 (£4,800 – £4,250) x 22%. Alternatively, under the normal rules, the tax liability would total £748 (£4,800 – £1,400) x 22%.

It is necessary to make an election if you want to adopt the simple method of paying Income Tax on the gross rents over £4,250 per annum.

Where an individual and some other person are entitled to income under the Rent-a-Room scheme the £4,250 limit is halved. Each lessor's exempt amount is then £2,125. This rule means that a married couple taking in lodgers should be able to arrange their affairs in such a way that the letting income is divisible between them (each spouse will then have a limit of £2,125); or goes wholly to either husband or wife (in which case either spouse will be due the full £4,250 limit).

Dividends and interest

The tables below set out the types of investment where the dividends and interest are paid to the investor:

- with a non-repayable tax credit;

- after deduction of Income Tax;

- no tax deducted.

Tax credit of 10%
Dividends on shares
Income distributions on unit trust holdings

Savings Income – Tax deducted at 20%
Building society interest
*Interest on British Government stocks, with some exceptions
Bank deposit interest
National Savings First Option Bonds
Purchased life annuities – income element

Savings Income – Interest not taxed at source
*Interest on British Government stocks
National Savings Bank ordinary and investment accounts
National Savings Income and Capital Bonds
National Savings Pensioners' Bonds
Certificates of Tax Deposit
Single deposits over £50,000 for a fixed period of not more than five years
Deposits with non-UK branches of banks and building societies

*You can receive interest on your investments in British Government stocks without tax of 20% deducted at source. However, if you are receiving your interest after deduction of tax, and you want your interest to be paid to you before tax in future, you will have to write and request this change in the way your interest is paid to you. Interest is always paid without deduction of tax at source on the following holdings:

INVESTMENT INCOME

- 3½% War Loan
- Government Stocks held on the National Savings Bank Register.

The various rates of tax you can end up paying on your dividend and interest income are set out in Chapter 1. These types of income are treated as the top part of your taxable income. If you have both dividend and savings income, the dividends must always be treated as the highest part. As a result it follows that:

- non-taxpayers will only be able to claim repayment of Income Tax on their savings income where tax at 20% has been deducted at source. The 10% tax credit on UK dividend income is non-repayable;
- individuals liable to Income Tax at only the 10% starting rate will be able to reclaim some of the tax at 20% suffered on their savings income;
- taxpayers who are liable at the basic rate of 22%, but not the top rate, will not face any further tax charge on their dividend and interest income; and
- individuals who are liable to tax at the top rate of 40% will be required to pay Income Tax of a further 20% each year to the extent that their non-dividend savings income takes them above the basic rate band and into the higher tax rate. Where the income beyond the basic rate band comes from UK dividends the extra tax payable is 22.5%.

Illustrations

1. Derek Bridge receives building society interest, including tax deducted at source, of £920 for 2002/03. His earned income, after allowances and reliefs, comes to £7,200. He pays tax for the year as follows:

On the first	£1,920 @ 10%
On the next	£5,280 @ 22%
On his interest income of	£920 @ 20%

2. Davina Wright banks interest and dividend income amounting to £4,300 and £2,800 (gross) respectively during 2002/03. Her earnings, after allowances and reliefs, total £26,500. Her tax charge is worked out as follows:

On the first	£1,920 @ 10%
On the next	£24,580 @ 22%
On her interest income of	£3,400 @ 20%
On her interest income of	£900 @ 40%
On her dividends	£2,800 @ 32.5%

ACCRUED INCOME

The £3,400 slice of interest income attracts tax at the rate of 20% as it falls within the limit of income of £29,900 taxed at the starting and basic rates.

Many people mistakenly assume – because the dividends and interest mentioned in the top two tables are paid after tax has been deducted – that they do not need to be reported on their annual Tax Return. This misunderstanding is most particularly associated with building society interest. Whatever the totals of your dividends and interest these details must be shown on your Tax Return. The amount of this income may be such as to give rise to a tax charge at the higher rate.

Individuals not liable to tax:

- can arrange to receive their interest gross. This is done by completing special forms which are available at banks, building societies, Post Offices and Tax Offices throughout the country;
- who receive interest from which tax has been deducted, can claim repayment from the Inland Revenue.

Both these measures particularly benefit non-earning married women, pensioners, children and other individuals not liable to Income Tax who choose to invest their savings in accounts with banks and building societies.

Accrued income

Interest on fixed-rate investments is treated as accruing on a day-to-day basis between payment dates. On a sale the vendor is charged to Income Tax on the accrued interest from the previous payment date to the date of the transaction. The purchaser is allowed to deduct this amount from the interest which he receives on the following payment date. These arrangements cover both fixed and variable-rate stocks and bonds, including those issued by governments, companies and local authorities. The arrangements will not affect you if the nominal value of your securities is under £5,000.

Illustration

The interest on a holding of 10% Treasury Stock 2004 is payable on each 18 May and 18 November. The half-yearly interest on a holding of £20,000, sold for settlement on 10 July 2002, is £1,000.

Accrued proportion = $53/183$ x £1,000 = £289.62

Offshore funds

You may have an investment in an Offshore Fund which distributes substantially all its income by way of dividend. If this is so then the regular dividends you receive are taxed as income and any profit or loss on sale will rank as either a capital gain or loss for the purposes of Capital Gains Tax (see Chapter 12).

Perhaps, however, the Fund pays no dividends and simply accumulates all the income it receives. Then, all the profit on sale is chargeable to Income Tax even if part of the gain could reasonably be considered to represent a capital profit.

Overseas investment income

Generally, income from investments abroad is considered to be income from savings like any other dividends or interest income. Any foreign tax paid can be deducted from the tax payable here on the same dividends or interest. If necessary you must be able to show that you have actually paid, or suffered, the overseas tax.

Non-qualifying life policies

Investment Bonds and Guaranteed Income Bonds offered by most life assurance companies fall within this category. A lump sum premium is paid at the outset. The investor can usually:

- make partial withdrawals from the Bond;
- draw an income; or
- leave it untouched until it is cashed in or forms part of his estate on death.

No tax relief is due on the single premium. The proceeds of a Bond are not liable to Capital Gains Tax or Income Tax at the basic rate. There can be a liability to tax at the difference between the higher and basic rates on chargeable events. These arise on:

- surrender or maturity of the policy;
- on death of the life assured; or
- on withdrawals in excess of the cumulative allowance built up at the time.

At the end of each policy year, an allowance of 5% of the original investment is given. This can be carried forward from year to year. It follows that over a period of 20 years allowances of up to 100% of the initial investment will be given. A taxable gain only arises if the amount of a withdrawal is more than the cumulative allowances at the time. It is the excess which is taxed.

Illustration

Edward Clark invests £8,000 in an Investment Bond. Withdrawals of £700 and £2,300 are made during the third and sixth policy years. The annual allowance is £400 being 5% of the original investment. A taxable gain of £600 arises in year six as follows:

NON-QUALIFYING LIFE POLICIES

Number of Policy Years	Cumulative Allowance £	Amount Withdrawn £	Cumulative Withdrawals £	Taxable Amount £
1	400	–	–	–
2	800	–	–	–
3	1,200	700	700	–
4	1,600	–	700	–
5	2,000	–	700	–
6	2,400	2,300	3,000	600

When the final chargeable event on a Bond occurs, the taxable gain is calculated by taking into account all previous withdrawals and taxable gains.

Illustration

The Investment Bond in the illustration above is encashed after nine years for £11,504. The taxable gain amounts to £5,904 as follows:

	£	£
Policy proceeds		11,504
Add: Withdrawals in years 3 and 6		3,000
		14,504
Less: Original investment	8,000	
Amount already taxed	600	
		8,600
Taxable gain on encashment		£5,904

The method of calculating the Income Tax due on the taxable gain involves a number of stages including *top slicing* relief.

Illustration

Edward Clark, who made a gain of £5,904 on the final encashment of his Investment Bond featured in the two earlier illustrations, is a single man. During 2002/03 his other income, all earnings, amounted to £34,400.

Gain on encashment of Bond	£5,904
Number of years held	9
Taxable slice of gain	£656
Taxable income – excluding slice of gain	£
Earnings	34,400
Less: Personal allowance	4,615
	£29,785

Tax applicable to slice of gain
  On first £115 (£29,900 – £29,785) @ 0%   –
  On next £541 (excess over £29,900)
    @18% (40% – 22%)   £97.38
Average rate on slice   14.84%
The tax payable on the gain =
  £5,904 @ 14.84% =   £876.15

Individual Savings Accounts

An Individual Savings Account (ISA) can include three components:

- cash (including National Savings);
- life assurance;
- stocks and shares.

You can subscribe to an ISA if you are:

- both resident and ordinarily resident in the UK for tax purposes; and
- aged 18 or over. 16- and 17-year-olds can invest in the cash component only.

The annual subscription limit is £7,000, of which no more than £3,000 can go into cash and £1,000 into life assurance. Other features of the ISA are:

- The account is completely free of tax.
- There is no statutory lock-in period or minimum subscription. Money can be withdrawn from an ISA whenever you like.
- There is no lifetime investment limit.
- A 10% tax credit will be paid for the first five years of the scheme, that is until 5 April 2004, on dividends from UK equity holdings.
- The scheme is guaranteed to run for at least ten years. It will be reviewed after seven years to decide on any changes after the initial ten-year term.
- Shares acquired under a public offer, or received when a building society or mutual insurer demutualizes, cannot be transferred into an ISA.

The list of qualifying investments allowed for the stocks and shares component of an ISA includes:

- Shares listed on a recognized Stock Exchange.
- Unit trusts.

TAX-EXEMPT SPECIAL SAVINGS ACCOUNTS

- Investment trusts.
- Open-ended investment companies.
- Government Stocks with at least five years to go to maturity.
- Share options exercised under an approved SAYE scheme.
- Qualifying Crown Depository Interests.

Each year savers will have two choices when it comes to appointing plan managers. The first option allows them to go to a single manager who must offer an account which can accept the overall subscription. This means that:

- the account must include the stocks and shares component, but does not need to offer either of the other two parts (cash and life assurance);
- savers will be able to subscribe up to £7,000 to the stocks and shares component;
- if, in addition, the manager offers the cash and/or life assurance parts, savers will be able to subscribe up to £3,000 to the cash component and £1,000 to the life assurance part, with the balance going into stocks and shares.

Under the second option savers can go to separate managers – one for each component – and subscribe:

- up to £3,000 in stocks and shares;
- £3,000 to cash; and
- £1,000 to life assurance.

These fixed individual limits will help to ensure that the overall annual investment limit can be satisfactorily monitored.

You will not need to include details of your ISA on your annual Tax Return.

Tax-Exempt Special Savings Accounts

A Tax-Exempt Special Savings Account (TESSA) is a saving scheme with a bank, building society or other institution where the interest is tax free. With the introduction of ISAs no new TESSA could be taken out after 5 April 1999. However, existing TESSAs can continue to run their course under existing rules:

- The account must run for the full five years.
- The freedom from Income Tax on the interest is lost if any part of the capital is withdrawn during the five-year investment period.

87

As TESSAs were primarily aimed to encourage the small saver the investment limit was relatively modest. Up to £9,000 may be invested over the five-year period. In the first year the maximum savings limit was £3,000. This reduces to £1,800 in each subsequent year but the overall limit of £9,000 must not be exceeded. Individuals can use a TESSA to make regular monthly savings or to deposit lump sums as and when they can. For example, both the following savings patterns are within the rules:

Year	Amount Invested £	£
1	3,000	2,200
2	1,800	1,800
3	1,800	None
4	1,800	1,500
5	600	1,800
	£9,000	£7,300

Any subscriptions after 5 April 1999 do not count towards the investment limits for an ISA. Investors can withdraw interest as it arises during the investment period. Up to the full amount of interest which has been credited to the account can be paid out at any time. However, an amount equivalent to the savings rate of Income Tax on the withdrawal must be retained within the TESSA. The Income Tax left in the account can be withdrawn in full at the end of the five-year period.

When a TESSA matures, savers can transfer their capital, but not accumulated interest, into the cash component of an ISA. Such a transfer does not affect the amount that can be subscribed to an ISA

If an investor dies during the period when the account is tax free, it comes to an end but none of the tax benefits up to that time are lost.

All the paperwork required by the Inland Revenue will be handled by the institution with which you have your TESSA. You will not need to mention the tax-free interest on your TESSA in your annual Tax Return.

Personal Equity Plans
Personal Equity Plans (PEPs) are a tax-free way of investing in shares. However, arising from the introduction of ISAs, no new money can be invested in PEPs after 5 April 1999. However, PEPs held at that date can continue under the present rules with the following benefits:

- Any dividends you receive on your UK equity holdings will receive a 10% tax credit for five years until 5 April 2004.

- There is no Capital Gains Tax to pay on profits made on selling shares within the plan.

- There are no tax penalties on withdrawing from, or closing down, a plan.

- You do not have to report your PEP dividend income and capital gains to the Inland Revenue on your annual Tax Return.

- The investments which can be held in a PEP are the same as those which are allowed for the stocks and shares component of an ISA.

Friendly Societies

All individuals, including children under 18, can invest up to £270 per annum in a tax-exempt savings plan with a Friendly Society. A family with two children can now save as much as £1,080 per annum through this type of investment.

Enterprise Investment Scheme

The aims of the Scheme are twofold:

- to provide a targeted incentive for equity investment in unquoted trading companies which will help overcome the problems faced by such companies in raising small amounts of equity finance;

- to encourage outside investors, who introduce finance and expertise to a company, by enabling them to take an active part in the management of the company as paid directors without losing entitlement to relief.

The main features of the Scheme are:

- Income Tax relief at 20% on qualifying investments up to £150,000 in any tax year;

- investors are allowed either Income Tax or Capital Gains Tax relief for losses made on the disposal of qualifying shares;

- all shares in a qualifying company must be held for at least three years;

- investors previously unconnected with a qualifying company or its trade can become directors whilst still eligible for relief on their investment;

- relief on up to one-half of the amount that an individual invests between 6 April and 5 October in any tax year can be carried back to the previous tax year, subject to a maximum limit of £25,000.

Venture Capital Trusts

The Venture Capital Trust Scheme is aimed at generating equity investment in dynamic, innovative, unquoted trading companies. The shares of Venture Capital Trusts must be quoted on the Stock Exchange. Individuals who invest in them are eligible for the following Income Tax incentives:

- relief at 20% on subscriptions up to £100,000 in any tax year for new ordinary shares providing the shares are held for at least three years;

- tax-free dividends.

Joint income

Many married couples have bank or building society accounts, Unit Trust Holdings or other share investments, or property held in their joint names. They are then treated as if they own the account or asset equally and each will have to pay Income Tax on half the annual income. Alternatively, if capital invested in a Building Society account in joint names actually belongs to husband and wife in unequal shares they can be taxed on their respective shares of the income. The married couple must then declare to the Inland Revenue how the account or other property and the income are shared between them. There is a special form to complete. The declaration applies from the date it is made.

Where one spouse transfers an income-producing asset to the other spouse knowing or expecting that the income will be credited to a joint account on which the donor spouse is free to draw, the income will still be regarded as belonging to the donor spouse for tax purposes.

10

THE FAMILY UNIT

Husbands and wives are taxed separately on their income and capital gains. They must complete their own Tax Returns every year and are each responsible for settling their respective tax liabilities.

Marriage

Husband and wife are each entitled to personal allowances which can be set against their own income each year, whether this be from earnings or from investments. They can each have taxable income, after allowances and reliefs, of £29,900 for 2002/03 before either of them is liable to tax at the higher 40% rate. They may, of course, need to make some rearrangements to their affairs if they are to take full advantage of opportunities to save tax.

Children

A child is treated as a separate individual for tax purposes like anyone else. A wage that your son or daughter receives, for example, for a weekend job in the local newsagent's shop is taxable. However, a child is also entitled to the personal allowance so no tax is probably payable on the earnings.

If all this tempts you to think about giving some of your savings to your children so that the Income Tax on the interest earned can be recovered by being set off against their personal allowances, then I must warn you to proceed with caution. The income from a gift by a parent in favour of an unmarried minor/child is regarded as the parent's income for tax purposes subject to an annual £100 limit for small amounts of income. This means that a married couple with two children can only give away capital which will generate up to £400 in income each year. Separate accounts should be opened for each child for the gifts from each parent. If, for some reason, the £100 limit is surpassed, the whole income – not just the excess over £100 – becomes taxable on the parent. Grandparents or other relatives can, however, give savings to their grandchildren or nieces, nephews, etc. without the same restrictions.

In the previous chapter (Chapter 9) on investment income I mentioned the following which will be of considerable benefit to children:

- interest on, for example, a National Savings Bank investment account is not taxed at source, unlike that on a bank or building society account where the interest is paid to the investor after deduction of tax at the savings rate;

- savers, such as children, who are not taxpayers can, however, elect to receive gross interest on their bank or building society investments.

As an alternative to a bank or building society account for your child's savings, why not take a look at the Children's Bonus Bonds issued by the Department for National Savings. They are particularly suitable for gifts from parents. The return on these bonds is exempt from both Income Tax and Capital Gains Tax. This tax exemption means that no parent can be liable to Income Tax on interest arising on the gift.

There is no general tax allowance for children. However:

- you should be able to claim child benefit and may be entitled to the new Children's Tax Credit (see chapter 2);
- depending on your personal circumstances you may be entitled to one or more of the numerous other social security benefits associated with children, but unfortunately it is outside the scope of this book to go into them in detail.

Responsibility for completing a minor's Income Tax Repayment Claim rests with the child's trustee or guardian. A minor child is also a taxable person for the purposes of Capital Gains Tax (Chapter 12) and Inheritance Tax (Chapter 16).

Separation and divorce

Not only can the breakdown of a marriage cause much personal suffering, particularly when there are children of the marriage, but invariably it also calls for a reorganisation of the parted couple's financial affairs. For the over 65s the married couple's allowance is still due in the year of separation.

Limited tax relief is available to payers of maintenance under Court Orders and Maintenance Agreements as follows:

- either the payer or recipient must be born before 6 April 1935;
- the payment must be to the divorced or separated spouse;
- the maximum amount of tax relief to which the payer is entitled is 10% of either £2,110 or, if less, the actual maintenance paid each year;
- no tax relief can be claimed on maintenance paid to, or for, children.

Maintenance payments are tax free in the hands of the recipient.

Old age

Unfortunately, the elderly taxpayer has to cope with the tax system in exactly the same way as everyone else. Nevertheless, there are some factors which are only relevant in calculating the tax payable on the elderly person's income. First and foremost are the age allowances. In Chapter 2 I explained how a pensioner calculates whether he or she is entitled to these allowances.

Pensions, apart from the war disablement and widow's pensions, are taxable. These include a pension from either the State, a retirement annuity, a personal pension or a past employer's fund. The State Pension includes:

- the basic retirement (or old person's) pension;
- a state earnings-related pension (SERPS);
- a graduated pension;
- the age addition if you are over 80.

Although it is taxable, no tax is deducted at source from the State Pension. In addition to including a pensioner's personal allowances in the coding notice of a pension taxed under PAYE it will also incorporate a deduction equivalent to the State Retirement Pension. In this way the tax due on it is collected. The need to make a direct tax payment is avoided.

The significance of the following letters at the end of a code number is as follows:

- V – indicates the pensioner is entitled to both the personal and married couple's allowances for ages 65–74 and is liable to tax at the basic rate;
- P – is for a code with the personal allowance for those aged 65–74;
- Y – is the code if you are due the personal allowance for age 75 and over; and
- T – applies in most other circumstances.

In the exceptional situation of the deduction for the State Retirement Pension exceeding a pensioner's personal allowances, the Inland Revenue issue a 'K' coding. The amount of the negative allowance is then added to your pension on which tax is to be paid.

When a person starts to draw the old age pension, the Department of Social Security sends out a form to find out the tax office which deals with the pensioner's Tax Return. This enables the Department to tell the tax office of the amount of a new pensioner's State Pension and subsequent increases. This makes sure the correct deduction for the State Pension is always included in a pensioner's code number.

With careful planning an elderly married couple with modest incomes may well be able to generate significant savings in their tax bills as the following example demonstrates.

Illustration

Gordon and Hilda Kelly, an elderly married couple, both in their early 70s, whose joint income for 2002/03 amounted to £35,000, paid Income Tax of £4,646.50 for the year. This all related to Gordon's income as follows:

THE FAMILY UNIT

	Gordon £	Hilda £
State Pensions	3,926	2,350
Occupational Pensions	11,234	2,550
Building Society Interest		
– Gross equivalent	9,000	–
Interest on British Government Stocks	4,840	1,100
	29,000	6,000
Less: Personal Allowance	4,615	6,100
Taxable Income	£24,385	£–
Income Tax Payable		
£1,920 @ 10%	192.00	–
£8,625 @ 22%	1,897.50	–
£13,840 @ 20% (savings income)	2,768.00	–
	4,857.50	–
Less: Relief for married couple's allowance – £2,110 @ 10%	211.00	–
	£4,646.50	£–

Gordon's income is above the upper limit beyond which he is not due either the personal age or married couple's allowances. Also Hilda has insufficient income to benefit from her full personal age allowance.

Significant tax savings of £878.40 for 2002/03 could have been achieved by the couple if Gordon had transferred capital to Hilda as follows:

	Gordon £	Hilda £
State Pensions	3,926	2,350
Occupational Pensions	11,234	2,550
Building Society Interest		
– Gross equivalent	2,000	7,000
Interest on British Government Stocks	640	5,300
	17,800	17,200
Less: Personal Allowance	6,110	6,110
Taxable Income	£11,690	£11,090

Income Tax Payable
£1,920 @ 10%	192.00	192.00
£7,130 @ 22%	1,568.60	–
£2,640/£9,170 @ 20% (savings income)	528.00	1,834.00
	2,288.60	2,026.00
Less: Relief for married couple's allowance – £5,465 @ 10%	546.50	–
	£1,742.10	£2,026.00

Death

Sadly, death comes to all of us and has consequences for taxation which are:

- there is no reduction in the married couple's allowance in the year of death of either spouse;

- if the husband dies first he is entitled to his full personal allowance in the year of death. If his income that year is such that he is unable to use up the full married couple's allowance then the balance can be transferred to his widow;

- where the wife dies before her husband she will be due the full personal or, if appropriate, personal age allowance in the year of death.

11

THE OVERSEAS ELEMENT

Apart from some special cases, the amount of tax you pay each year depends on whether you are resident in the United Kingdom (UK) and, to a lesser extent, on your domicile status. If you live permanently in the UK then, generally, all your income arising in this country will be liable to UK taxation. Overseas income is similarly taxable although special rules apply in taxing foreign income of individuals resident, but not domiciled, in the UK.

Not only are the two concepts of domicile and residence of fundamental importance in determining the extent of an individual's liability to UK taxation on income, they are of equal significance for the purposes of both Capital Gains Tax and Inheritance Tax.

Domicile

Your domicile will generally be considered to be the country or state which you regard as your permanent homeland. Your domicile is separate from your residence or nationality. When you are born you acquire a domicile of origin from your father. You can abandon your original domicile by birth if you settle in another country or state with a view to making it your new permanent home. Providing you sever all links with your current country of domicile you can move towards acquiring a domicile of choice in the new country. You should be prepared to provide a substantial amount of evidence that you propose to live there for ever.

A wife's domicile is not necessarily the same as her husband's domicile if they were married at some time after the end of 1973. It is decided by the same factors as for any other individual who is able to have an independent domicile. A woman who married before the beginning of 1974 automatically acquired the domicile of her husband on marriage. So long as the marriage lasts, her domicile only alters when there is any change in the domicile of her husband.

If you think you have good grounds for believing that you should not be regarded as domiciled in the UK you should write to your tax office about this. Usually, you can then expect to receive a questionnaire which you should fill in and send back to your tax office. The information you have supplied will be considered by the Inland Revenue Specialist Department which deals with these matters. In due course you will receive a ruling on your domicile status.

Residence and ordinary residence

There is no statutory definition of residence and ordinary residence. Each case must be judged on the facts. What follows is a summary of the main factors which will be taken into account.

Without exception you will always be regarded as resident in the UK if you spend 183 days or more here in the tax year. Days of arrival in, and departure from, the UK are normally left out of account in working out the number of days spent here.

If you are here for less than 183 days you will still be treated as resident where you visit the UK regularly and after four tax years your visits during those years average 91 days or more in a tax year. From the fifth year you are treated as a UK resident.

You are also regarded as ordinarily resident in the UK if you are resident here from year to year. It is possible to be resident, but not ordinarily resident. For example, you may normally live outside the UK but are in this country for at least 183 days in a tax year. Conversely you can occasionally be considered to be ordinarily resident, but not actually resident, for a particular tax year. This could happen if you live in the UK but, for some reason, are abroad for a complete tax year.

Calculating annual average visits

The set formula to be used in working out the average number of days spent in the UK each year is:

$$\frac{\text{total visits to the UK (in days)}}{\text{total period since leaving (in days)}} \times 365 \text{ days} = \text{annual average visits}$$

The maximum period over which the average is taken is four years.

Illustration

Thomas Winter, a retired solicitor, left the UK on 23 November 1999. In the period from the date of his departure to 5 April 2000 he visited the UK for 43 days. In the following three tax years to 5 April 2003, he spent 110, 85 and 57 days in the UK. The average number of days in the UK works out at 87.61 as follows:

$$\frac{43 + 110 + 85 + 57}{133 + 365 + 366 + 365} = \frac{295}{1,229} \times 365 = 87.61 \text{ days}$$

As this is less than the 91 days per annum average Thomas will be treated as non-resident throughout the period.

Working abroad – long absences

Poor job prospects in the UK, together with higher salaries and low taxation abroad, may prompt you to look for work overseas. This is likely to involve living abroad permanently for a time. Your probable residence status is clearly set out in paragraphs 2:2 and 2:3 of the Inland Revenue booklet IR20 – *Residents and Non-Residents* – as follows:

If you leave the UK to work full time abroad under a contract of employment, you are treated as not resident and not ordinarily resident if you meet all the following conditions:

- your absence from the UK and your employment abroad both last for at least a whole tax year;

- during your absence any visits you make to the UK
  - total less than 183 days in any tax year, and
  - average less than 91 days a tax year (the average is taken over the period of absence up to a maximum of four years; any dates spent in the UK because of exceptional circumstances beyond your control, for example the illness of yourself or a member of your immediate family, are not normally counted for this purpose).

Should you meet all of the above conditions you are treated as not resident and not ordinarily resident in the UK from the day after you leave the UK to the date before you return to the UK at the end of your employment abroad. You are treated as coming to the UK permanently on the day you return from your employment abroad and as resident and ordinarily resident from that date.

There will be no tax to pay here on your salary for the part of the tax year after you have left the UK.

There is no specific definition of when employment abroad is 'full time'. Each particular case must be considered on all the facts. Nevertheless, where your employment involves a standard pattern of hours, it will be regarded as full time if your working hours each week are comparable with those that would be worked in the UK. Furthermore, several part-time jobs all at the same time could be taken as constituting full-time employment.

If you leave the UK to work full time in a trade, profession or vocation overseas and fulfil the same conditions as anyone taking up full-time employment abroad then your UK residence status will be determined in the same way.

You may well take your spouse with you. By concession he or she may also be regarded as neither resident nor ordinarily resident for the same period even if your spouse does not work abroad.

Working abroad – expenses

Tax relief is allowed on travel expenses you incur in relation to your overseas employment. Nor will you be taxed on the cost of board and lodging provided for you where the expenses are borne by your employer.

Generally, whenever your job takes you overseas, even for short periods, you will not be taxed on the cost of your travelling expenses so long as your employer meets the bills. This also applies to the costs of unlimited return visits to the UK during longer assignments abroad.

No taxable benefit arises where your employer meets the travelling costs of your spouse and children to visit you overseas. Not more than two return visits by the same person are allowed each year, and you must be working abroad for a continuous period of at least 60 days.

Leaving the UK permanently

Where you go abroad to live permanently, or to live outside the UK for three years or more, you will provisionally be considered neither resident nor ordinarily resident in the UK from the day following your departure. You should be prepared to provide sufficient evidence of your intention to make a permanent home somewhere outside the UK. Providing you do not infringe the rules about visits to the UK the provisional non-resident ruling will subsequently be confirmed by the Inland Revenue. You are entitled to full allowances and reliefs for the year of departure.

Before you leave, ask your tax office for the special form (P85) to be completed by individuals going abroad. The information in the form about your intended residence position will enable the Inland Revenue to make an in-year tax refund to you if, for example, you are claiming split-year treatment.

When you become not ordinarily resident in the UK you can apply to receive interest on any bank or building society account here without deduction of tax. Similarly, Income Tax is not charged on the interest from certain UK Government Securities.

Allowances for non-UK residents

You may be able to claim UK tax allowances if you are not resident here. If you are eligible to claim you will generally be entitled to the same allowances as an individual resident in the UK. The following individuals can claim:

- a citizen of the Commonwealth;
- a citizen of a state within the European Union;
- a present or former employee of the British Crown;
- a resident of the Isle of Man or the Channel Islands;
- certain other specific classes of individuals.

Income from UK property

Many individuals choose to rent out their homes while they are away, particularly when they go to work abroad. You can apply to the Inland Revenue for a certificate authorizing your tenant, or managing agent, to make payments of rent to you without deducting UK tax. If no such certificate is issued, tax at the basic rate must be withheld from all remittances of rent to you.

Even though you are not resident in the UK you could still be liable to UK tax on income arising from the letting out of UK property. This is so, whether or not tax is deducted by your tenant or letting agent. However, you will not actually have any UK tax to pay if your total income, including your income from property after allowable expenses, chargeable to UK tax is less than any allowances which you may be entitled to claim.

Double taxation relief

If you move to a country with which the UK has concluded a Double Taxation Agreement, you may be able to claim partial or full exemption from UK tax on certain types of income from UK sources. Normally, you should be entitled to some measure of relief from UK tax on pensions and annuities, royalties and dividends. Many Double Taxation Agreements contain clauses dealing with the special circumstances of teachers and researchers, students and apprentices, and entertainers and sportsmen/women.

Going abroad – Capital Gains Tax

If you have been resident in the UK for at least four out of the last seven years ending with the day you leave and, within five years, you return here to take up residence for tax purposes again, then the concessionary split-year tax treatment does not apply for the purposes of Capital Gains Tax. You will be classified as a UK resident for the entire tax years of both departure and return.

It follows that gains realized in the tax year of departure will be taxed in that year. All gains in subsequent years, including the year of return, will be subject to Capital Gains Tax in the year when residence resumes. Profits made on assets bought and sold during the years of non-UK tax residence will not, however, be liable to Capital Gains Tax in the UK.

Taking up UK residence

Perhaps you have been working overseas, your contract has come to an end and you are thinking about returning here. Before you take up UK residence again there are some specific tax-planning points which must be considered. For example, any bank deposit or building society accounts should be closed before you return as you could otherwise face the prospect of a charge to UK Income Tax on interest accrued, but not credited, during your period of non-residence.

If the UK is not your normal homeland you should initially be able to satisfy our Inland Revenue Authorities that you have an overseas domicile. Any income from investments here is taxable as it arises. Your overseas investment income is not taxed unless it is actually remitted or enjoyed here. Where your job is with either a UK or an overseas employer, and the duties of your employment are performed wholly in the UK, the full amount of your salary is taxable here. Table 8 at the end of the book is a summary of the scope of liability to Income Tax of earnings.

You will be treated as resident and ordinarily resident from the date you arrive if you are either coming here permanently or intending to stay for at least three years. You will be able to claim full UK personal allowances for the year of arrival.

You should let the Inland Revenue know when you come to the UK. You will normally be asked to complete a form P86 which will help to determine your residence status. The form also includes a section on domicile so that it will be possible, in straightforward cases, to deal with both your residence status and domicile together. This will apply, for example, if you:

- have never been domiciled within the UK;

- have come here only to work; and

- intend to leave the UK once your employment ceases.

In less straightforward cases where domicile affects liability to UK taxation, you will need to obtain another form in order to give the further information necessary to determine your domicile.

12

CAPITAL GAINS TAX

As its name implies, Capital Gains Tax is a tax on profits you realize from the disposal of capital assets. As with most other forms of taxation there is the usual list of exceptions to this general rule. Gambling, pools or lottery winnings, personal or professional damages and mortgage cashbacks are not taxable. Neither are gains realized on disposing of any of the assets in the following table:

- private cars

- National Savings

- your private residence

- chattels, with an expected life of more than 50 years, sold for less than £6,000

- British government securities and many corporate bonds

- shares issued under the Business Expansion Scheme after 18 March 1986 on their first disposal

- shares issued under the Enterprise Investment Scheme on their first disposal, so long as the tax relief has not been withdrawn

- shares in Venture Capital Trusts

- investments in a Personal Equity Plan

- investments in an Individual Savings Account

- life assurance policies – unless purchased by you

- charitable gifts

- gifts for the public benefit

- foreign currency for personal expenditure.

The list of taxable gains includes profits made from disposing of property, shareholdings, unit trust holdings, works of art and foreign currency for other than personal expenditure.

Rate of tax

For the 2002/03 tax year the first £7,700 of chargeable gains you realize are tax free. Gains in excess of the annual tax-free allowance are charged at your Income Tax rates found by adding the gains to your taxable income.

Illustration

Isaac Woolf realized gains of £18,000 during 2002/03. His taxable income, after personal allowances and reliefs, was £24,000. The Capital Gains Tax he owes for the year is £2,940 as follows:

	£
Realized gains	18,000
Less: Exemption limit	7,700
	£10,300
Tax payable:	
£5,900 @ 20% (Savings Rate)	1,180
£4,400 @ 40%	1,760
2002/03 Capital Gains Tax payable	£2,940

The amount of Capital Gains Tax at 20% is worked out on the difference between the £29,900 limit of income taxable at the starting and basic rates and Isaac's income of £24,000.

Any allowances or reliefs which you are unable to use because your income is too low cannot be set against your capital gains.

Married couples

Husband and wife are:

- Each entitled to the annual exemption limit.

- Taxed separately on the chargeable gains they realize in the tax year above the annual exemption limit.

A married couple living together can transfer assets between them free of tax. Assets are regarded as passing from one spouse to the other without either gain or loss. For tax purposes the recipient is deemed to have acquired such assets at the other spouse's cost. The exemption from taxing gains on transfers between spouses ceases when a couple permanently separates.

In cases where a married couple hold an asset in their joint names, any gain is apportioned between them in the ratio of their respective interests in the asset at the time of disposal. This treatment may not necessarily follow the split of the income for income tax purposes. Here the law generally assumes a married couple are equally entitled to the income even if, in fact, this is not so. Where a couple have jointly made a declaration to the Inland Revenue of the ratio in which an asset and the income derived from it are shared between them, the same split will follow for Capital Gains Tax purposes.

Losses
Losses can be set against gains made in the same tax year. Unused losses can be carried forward to be set against gains in subsequent tax years without time limit. They then reduce the amount of your gains in excess of the annual exemption limit.

Illustration
Sally Rogers had capital losses of £5,200 available for carry-forward at 5 April 2002. During 2002/03 she realized gains of £9,800 and made losses of £900.

Her capital gains position for the year is:

	£	£
Gains realized in the year		9,800
Less: Losses: in the year	900	
brought forward (part)	1,200	
		2,100
2002/03 Exemption limit		£7,700

The unused losses of £4,000 can be carried forward to be set against gains in later years.

Losses realized by one spouse cannot be set against gains realized by the other spouse. This restriction on the set-off of losses also extends to unused losses at 5 April 1990.

A loss:
- arising on the sale or gift of an investment to a person connected with the individual making the disposal can only be set off against a gain from a similar disposal at a later date;

- can be claimed where the value of an asset you own becomes negligible or nil. You do not actually have to dispose of the asset. The loss arises on the date that the relief is claimed. In practice, however, a two-year period is allowed from the end of the tax year in which the asset became of negligible value;

- on shares you subscribe for in a trading company not quoted on a recognized Stock Exchange can be set against your income, rather than against other capital gains. This applies whether you realize a loss on disposing of such shares, or they become worthless.

The computation of gains

The taxable gain on the disposal of an asset is calculated by making various deductions from the sale proceeds, as follows:

- the cost of acquisition, and

- the incidental costs of buying and selling the asset, and

- any additional expenditure incurred on enhancing the value of the asset during the period of ownership, and

- the indexation allowance.

There are occasions when a different figure from the actual disposal proceeds is substituted in the calculation. For example, this happens when you make a gift or sell an asset at a nominal value to a close member of your family. You must then bring into the computation of the capital gain the open-market value of the asset at the time of disposal.

The date of sale of an asset is taken as the date when the contract for sale is made. The same rule determines the date of acquisition.

Later on in this chapter I shall deal with the special rules in cases where you dispose of assets you owned on either 31 March 1982 or 6 April 1965.

The indexation allowance

This allowance, which has now been frozen, measures the impact of inflation on both the cost of an asset and any other expenditure you have incurred on enhancing its value. The rules dealing with the calculation of the allowance are:

- the allowance is governed by the movement in the Retail Prices Index in the period of ownership up to April 1998. For assets which you have owned since before April 1982 the starting date for calculating the indexation allowance is March 1982;

- when you dispose of an asset which you acquired before 6 April 1982 the indexation allowance can be calculated on either the market value of the asset at 31 March 1982 or its actual cost, whichever is greater. Where you elect for the capital gains on all disposals of assets which you owned on 31 March 1982 to be worked out on their values at that date, ignoring original costs, the indexation allowance can only be calculated on those values;

- the allowance will not be given where an asset is sold at a loss. Neither can the indexation allowance turn a gain into a loss. It can only serve to reduce a gain to nil.

No indexation allowance is allowed in working out the chargeable gain on assets which are acquired on or after 1 April 1998. For disposals of assets acquired previously the indexation allowance is given for periods up to April 1998, but not thereafter.

Table 9 at the end of the book sets out the indexation allowance for April 1998. It is not possible in the space permitted to reproduce previous indexation allowance tables. If you need this information you should approach the tax office responsible for your tax affairs.

Illustration

A freehold property was purchased in November 1987 for £40,000. The legal fees and stamp duty on the purchase came to £1,340. An extension was added in February 1990 at a cost of £9,400.

Contracts for sale were exchanged in November 2002. It was sold for £96,000. The estate agents' commission, including the costs of advertising, and solicitors' fees, came to £2,820.

The indexation allowance between November 1987 and April 1998 is 0.573, and from February 1990 to April 1998 is 0.353.

The chargeable gain, before taper relief, is £15,435 as follows:

	£	£
Sale price		96,000
Less: Costs of sale		2,820
		93,180

Less:	Acquisition price	40,000	
	Costs of purchase	1,340	
	Enhancement expenditure		
	– extension	9,400	
		50,740	
	Indexation allowance:		
	£41,340 × 0.573	23,687	
	£9,400 × 0.353	3,318	
			77,745
	Chargeable gain, before taper relief		£15,435

Taper relief

Chargeable gains are subject to taper relief, the replacement for the indexation allowance. The main features of taper relief are:

- The proportion of a chargeable gain brought in to charge to tax is reduced by reference to the number of whole years (up to a maximum of ten) that an asset has been held.

- For this purpose a year is any continuous period of 12 months.

- Fractions of a year are ignored.

- There are two different percentage tables, one for business assets and one for non-business assets. The reductions for business assets are far more generous than those for non-business assets.

Gains on business assets

Number of whole years in qualifying holding period	Percentage of gain chargeable
1	50
2	25
3	25
4	25
5	25
6	25
7	25
8	25
9	25
10 or more	25

Gains on non-business assets

Number of whole years in qualifying holding period	Percentage of gain chargeable
1	100
2	100
3	95
4	90
5	85
6	80
7	75
8	70
9	65
10 or more	60

For the purpose of these rules the qualifying holding period for an asset is the time between:

- The later of the date of acquisition and 6 April 1998, and
- The date of disposal.

The qualifying holding period is increased by one year for a non-business asset which was acquired before 17 March 1998.

While indexation was deducted in working out the amount of a gain, taper relief is given after the chargeable gain has been calculated. Thus, in a case where a chargeable gain arises on a disposal to which both frozen indexation allowance and taper relief apply:

- The indexation allowance is first of all taken off to arrive at the amount of gain;
- Any allowable losses are deducted from the gain;
- Finally, taper relief is based on the net amount of the gain.

Allowable losses are not tapered. They are set off against chargeable gains before taper relief. The treatment is similar for both losses made in the same tax year as well as those brought forward from earlier years. By deducting losses from gains, before applying the taper, means that both losses and gains are effectively subjected to taper relief. Nevertheless, you can set losses against gains for this purpose in order to achieve the lowest possible tax charge. This means setting them:

- first against any gains on which no taper relief is available;
- then against any gains where the taper relief is less than on other gains, and so on.

Illustration

Andrew Walton bought shares in a quoted company, for which he does not work, in April 1993 for £5,100. He sold the shares in February 2003 for £18,900. In 2002/03 Andrew also realized a loss of £2,600 on the disposal of another asset.

The indexation allowance between April 1993 and April 1998 is 0.156.

Andrew's net chargeable gain for 2002/03 is £8,845 as follows:

ASSETS OWNED ON 31 MARCH 1982

	£	£
Sale proceeds of shares		18,900
Less: Cost price	5,100	
Indexation allowance 0.156	795	
		5,895
		13,005
Less: Loss on sale of other asset		2,600
		10,405
Less: Taper relief – 15%		1,560
Net chargeable gain		£8,845

Andrew owned the shares for four complete tax years after 5 April 1998. As he bought the shares before 17 March 1998, Andrew benefits from a bonus year and is entitled to five years of non-business assets taper relief.

Assets owned on 31 March 1982

Gains and losses on disposals of assets which you owned on 31 March 1982 can be calculated solely by reference to their market value at that date, ignoring original costs. In most cases, these rules will mean your capital gains are reduced compared with the calculation based on historical cost only.

Illustration

A freehold property purchased in 1976 for £20,000 was sold in October 2002 for £84,000. At 31 March 1982 it was valued at £38,000. The indexation allowance between March 1982 and April 1998 is 1.047.

The chargeable gain is £5,282 as follows:

	On 31 March 1982 Value			On Historical Cost
	£	£	£	£
Sale price		84,000		84,000
Less: March 1982 value	38,000		–	
Acquisition cost	–		20,000	
Indexation allowance				
£38,000 x 1.047	39,786		39,786	
		77,786		59,786
		£6,214		£24,214
Lesser gain			6,214	
Less: Taper relief – 15%			932	
2002/03 chargeable gain			£5,282	

Needless to say, there are special rules where the calculations based firstly on the March 1982 value and secondly on historical cost give different results, as follows:

On March 1982 Value	On Historical Cost	Chargeable Gain/Loss
Gain of £3,810	Gain of £2,150	£2,150 Gain
Loss of £515	Loss of £95	£95 Loss
Loss of £490	Gain of £760	neither gain nor loss
Gain of £2,435	Loss of £1,640	neither gain nor loss

You can, however, elect for the capital gains on all disposals of assets which you owned on 31 March 1982 to be worked out by reference to their values at that date, ignoring original costs. Once made, the election cannot be revoked.

Quoted stocks and shares

Prior to 6 April 1982 each shareholding was regarded as a single asset. This was commonly known as a 'pool'. Each additional purchase of the same class of shares or a sale of part of the holding represented either an addition to, or a disposal out of, the pool. With the introduction of the indexation allowance this changed. Each shareholding acquired after 5 April 1982 represented a separate asset. A subsequent addition to a holding you owned at 5 April 1982 could not be added to the pool.

The rules were altered from 6 April 1985. Shares of the same class were again regarded as a single asset growing or diminishing on each acquisition or disposal. This form of 'pooling' applied to shares acquired after 5 April 1982 unless they had already been disposed of before 6 April 1985; it is called a 'new holding'. A pool which was frozen under the 1982 rules stays that way. It remains a single asset which cannot grow by subsequent acquisitions and is known as a '1982 holding'.

A '1982 holding' is treated like any other asset in calculating the indexation allowance. This is not so for a 'new holding'. It had to be kept continually indexed each time there was an addition to, or a disposal out of, the pool up until April 1998.

The introduction of taper relief means that 'pooling' ceases for acquisitions of shares on or after 6 April 1998. This is necessary since the date of each acquisition needs to be recorded and retained.

The procedure for matching shares sold with their corresponding acquisition is as follows:

- shares acquired on the same day;

QUOTED STOCKS AND SHARES

- shares acquired within 30 days following a disposal;
- shares acquired before the disposal, but after 5 April 1998, identifying the most recent acquisitions first;
- shares comprised in a 'new holding', the 1982–1998 share pool;
- shares within a '1982 holding', the 1965–1982 share pool;
- any shares acquired before 6 April 1965, last in first out;
- shares acquired more than 30 days after the disposal.

Illustration

Lauren Dawson bought 2,000 shares in a quoted company on 9 September 1995 at a total cost of £2,200. She sold the entire holding on 27 November 2002 for £3,400. She then went on to reacquire the same number of shares in the company on 6 December 2002 for £3,150.

As the repurchase took place within 30 days of the sale the profit on the disposal is:

	£
Sale of 2,000 shares on 27 November 2002	3,400
Less: Cost of reacquisition on 6 December 2002	3,150
Chargeable gain	£250

Illustration

Gareth Davies made the following purchases in the shares of a quoted company:

Date	Number of Shares	Cost
May 1974	1,500	£1,875
Jan 1981	2,500	£3,500
Mar 1985	3,000	£3,900
Feb 1988	1,000	£1,700
June 1998	2,000	£5,600

In March 2003 he sold 9,000 shares for £32,400. The shares were valued at £1.50 each on 31 March 1982. The indexation allowance is:

1.047 between March 1982 and April 1998
0.117 between March 1985 and February 1988
0.568 between February 1988 and April 1998

2,000 shares sold must first of all be identified with the acquisition after 5 April 1998 as follows:

	£
Cost of 2,000 shares in June 1998	5,600
Proceeds of sale of 2,000 shares	7,200
	1,600
Less: Taper relief – 10%	160
Chargeable gain	1,440

Secondly, 4,000 shares sold must be identified with those in the 'new holding' as follows:

	£
Cost of 3,000 shares in March 1985	3,900
Indexation allowance to February 1988 – 0.117	456
	4,356
Cost of 1,000 shares in February 1988	1,700
	6,056
Indexation allowance to April 1998 – 0.568	3,439
	9,495
Proceeds of sale of 4,000 shares	14,400
	4,905
Less: Taper relief – 15%	735
Chargeable gain	£4,170

The remaining 3,000 shares sold are then identified with part of the shares acquired before 31 March 1982. As the average cost is £1.34 per share it is beneficial to base the capital gain on the share price at 31 March 1982 as follows:

	£
Value of 3,000 shares at March 1982	4,500
Indexation allowance to April 1998 – 1.047	4,711
	9,211
Proceeds of sale of 3,000 shares	10,800
	1,589
Less: Taper relief – 15%	238
Chargeable gain	£1,351

The total chargeable gain on the sale is £6,961.

Whenever you receive a bonus issue of shares of the same class as an existing holding the date of their acquisition is the same as that of the original holding. The same principle applies to further shares acquired under a rights issue.

Where a company in which you have a holding is taken over and you receive:

- shares in the new company in exchange for your shares in the company taken over, no disposal takes place at that time. Your new holding is regarded as having been acquired at the same time, and for the same price, as the old one;

- a mixture of cash and shares in the new company, a gain or loss arises on the cash element of the take-over. It is then necessary to apportion the cost price of the old shares, including any indexation allowance up to the date of the take-over, between the cash received and the value of the shareholding in the new company at the time.

Unquoted investments

Many of the rules dealing with quoted stocks and shares also apply to computations on disposals of unquoted investments. For example, the indexing rules apply in the same way as they do to quoted shares.

Most of the special rules dealing with unquoted investments apply to assets held at 6 April 1965 when Capital Gains Tax was introduced.

Assets held on 6 April 1965

Following the introduction of rules dealing with assets owned on 31 March 1982, the special rules for assets held on 6 April 1965 are likely to be of less significance.

The method of computation:

- is known as 'time-apportionment';
- does not apply to quoted stocks and shares, only to unquoted investments and other assets such as land;
- is designed to eliminate from the charge to tax the profit on sale attributable to the period up to 5 April 1965;
- achieves this result by assuming that the asset increased in value at a standard rate throughout the period of ownership.

It is the gain, net of indexaton, that is time-apportioned. For assets acquired before 6 April 1945 time-apportionment benefit is limited to 20 years.

Instead of relying on the time-apportionment method, a taxpayer can make an irrevocable election for the value of the asset on 6 April 1965 to be substituted in a calculation of the capital gain arising on sale.

Illustration

A property purchased in June 1959 for £5,000 was sold in late April 2002 for £45,000. An election for the 6 April 1965 value is not beneficial. At 31 March 1982 it was worth £20,000. The indexation allowance between March 1982 and April 1998 is 1.047.

The first calculation of the chargeable gain is:

	£
Sale proceeds	45,000
Less: Purchase price	5,000
Gross gain	40,000
Less: Indexation allowance £20,000 x 1.047	20,940
Indexed gain	£19,060

Time-apportionment:

$$\frac{\text{April 1965 to April 2002} = 444 \text{ months}}{\text{June 1959 to April 2002} = 514 \text{ months}} \times £19,060 = £16,464$$

The second calculation of the chargeable gain is:

	£	£
Sale proceeds		45,000
Less: 31 March 1982 value	20,000	
Indexation allowance £20,000 x 1.047	20,940	
		40,940
		£4,060

It is advantageous for the 31 March 1982 value to be used in calculating the chargeable gain, which is £4,060, subject to taper relief.

For quoted shares and securities held at 6 April 1965:

- a taxpayer can elect for the capital gains to be calculated by substituting the 6 April 1965 values for the original costs in all cases;
- separate elections must be made for the taxpayer and spouse and they are required both for ordinary shares and for fixed-interest securities;

- the election for each category is irrevocable and has to be made within two years of the end of the tax year in which the first sale after 19 March 1968 occurs;

- if no election is made the capital gain is worked out by comparing the disposal proceeds with the original cost and value of the holding on 6 April 1965.

Where, as is more likely, a taxpayer has elected for the capital gains on disposals of all assets owned on 31 March 1982 to be worked out solely by reference to their values at that date, the above rules setting out the alternatives available for assets held on 6 April 1965 will be superseded.

Valuations

If you need to use any valuations to work out the gain or loss on a disposal, there is a free service from the Inland Revenue to help you to complete your Self-Assessment Tax Return.

You:

- may ask your Tax Office to check valuations after you have made the disposal but before you make your Return;

- can ask for one copy of form CG34 for each valuation you want checked;

- must then send back the completed form to your Tax Office together with all the other information and documents requested on the form.

If your valuations are agreed they will not subsequently be challenged when you submit your Tax Return unless there are important facts affecting the valuations that you did not mention. If your figures are not agreed the Inland Revenue will put forward alternative valuations.

Your private residence

The profit on a sale of your home is exempt from tax. The exemption extends to the house and its garden or grounds up to half a hectare, including the land on which the house is built. A larger area can qualify for exemption where it can be shown that it was needed to enjoy the house.

Where a home has not been occupied as your private residence throughout the full period of ownership, or, if later, since 31 March 1982, a proportion of the gain on sale becomes taxable. Nevertheless, certain periods of absence are disregarded in determining whether the gain is totally exempt from tax. These are:

- the last three years of ownership in any event; and
- generally those when you have to live away from home because of your work.

Illustration
Ben White realized a capital gain of £68,000 when he sold his home in December 2002. It had been acquired back in May 1993. He was employed abroad between October 1993 and February 1995. In March 1999 he moved out into his new home.

Both the time spent working overseas and the last three years are regarded as periods when the home was Ben's main residence. The chargeable period is, therefore, only nine months and the chargeable gain, before taper relief, is £5,321 as follows:

$$\frac{\text{Chargeable period}}{\text{Period of ownership}} = \frac{9 \text{ months}}{115 \text{ months}} \times £68,000 = £5,321$$

Where part of your home is used exclusively for business purposes the proportion of the profit on sale attributable to the business use is a chargeable gain. Whether part of your home is actually used exclusively for business use is entirely a matter of fact.

If you let all or part of your home as residential accommodation, the gain on the part which has been let is either wholly or partly exempt from tax. The proportion of the profit on sale which is exempt is the lower of:

- either £40,000; or
- an amount equivalent to the gain on the part you have occupied as your home.

Illustration
Bill Gray made a capital gain of £94,000 when he disposed of his home in November 2002. It had been bought in June 1996. Bill and his family lived there until October 1996 and from October 1999 up to the date of sale. In the intervening period it was let. This period of absence was not one when the home was still regarded as Bill's main residence.

The chargeable gain is only £3,357 as follows:

	£	£
Capital gain (period of ownership – 77 months)		94,000
Less: Main residence exemption – 41 months	50,051	
Letting exemption – 36 months (lower of £40,000 or £50,051)	40,000	
		90,051
		3,949
Less: Taper relief – 15%		592
Chargeable gain		£3,357

Alternatively, if you take in lodgers who mix in and eat with your family, the Inland Revenue take the view that no part of the exemption on a sale of your home is lost. Nor should any capital gain arise if you take advantage of the Rent-a-Room scheme mentioned in Chapter 9.

A second home

If you have two homes such as a house or flat in town for use during the weekdays and a cottage in the country for weekends, the profit on sale of only one of them is exempt from tax. Which one counts as your main residence is a matter of fact. It is, however, possible for you to determine this by writing to your tax office. In the election you should request which of your homes you want regarded as your principal private residence for Capital Gains Tax purposes. The election:

- should apply from the date when you first have at least two homes available to you;
- can be made at any time in the two years beginning with the date from which it is to apply;
- can be varied as and when it suits you.

Husband and wife living together are only allowed one qualifying home between them.

If you own a home which was occupied rent free by the same dependent relative both on 5 April 1988 and throughout your period of ownership, then the profit on sale is tax free. Otherwise, it is likely that part of the gain will be taxable.

Chattels

Gains on the sales of chattels with an expected life of more than 50 years sold for less than £6,000 are exempt from tax. Chattels include paintings and other works of art, antiques, furniture, jewellery, stamps and ornaments. Articles comprising a set are regarded as a single item when they are sold to the same person but at different times.

For items which fetch between £6,000 and £15,000 the chargeable gain is restricted to $^5/_3$ times the amount of the proceeds of sale (ignoring expenses) over £6,000 where this is to the taxpayer's advantage.

Illustration

A piece of antique furniture purchased in January 1989 for £2,300 was sold at auction in June 2002 for £8,700, after expenses of sale were deducted.

The indexation allowance between January 1989 and April 1998 is 0.465. The chargeable gain is £3,825 as follows:

	£	£
Sale Price		8,700
Less: Purchase price	2,300	
Indexation allowance 0.465	1,070	3,370
Gain		£5,330
But restricted to 5/3 × £2,700 (£8,700 – £6,000)		4,500
Less: Taper Relief – 15%		675
Chargeable gain		£3,825

Where an article is sold at a loss for under £6,000, the allowable loss is restricted by assuming the proceeds on sale were equivalent to £6,000.

Illustration

A painting was purchased many years ago for £10,400. It was sold in March 2003 for £7,500. The allowable loss is £2,900. If it had fetched £4,000 on sale, the allowable loss would only be £4,400 (£10,400 – £6,000).

Wasting assets

Wasting assets are assets with an expected life span of less than 50 years. Unless it comes within the definition of 'tangible moveable property' a gain on the sale of a wasting asset is calculated in the same way as that on the sale of any other asset, except that the purchase price wastes away during the asset's expected life span. Leases of land for less than 50 years are wasting assets. A specific table is provided for calculating the proportion of the purchase price of a lease which can be deducted from the sale proceeds.

The gain on a sale of a wasting asset which is also 'tangible moveable property' is exempt from tax. Neither does a loss on a sale of similar property count as an allowable loss.

Part disposals

Where you only sell part of an asset:

- its acquisition cost is apportioned between the part sold and the proportion retained. This is done on a pro-rata basis by reference to the proceeds of sale of the part sold and the open-market value of the proportion retained;

- any indexation allowance is calculated on the cost of the part sold;

- the proportion of the original cost of the asset attributable to the part which was not sold can be set against the proceeds on a sale of the remainder at a later date. This calculation must be reworked on the 31 March 1982 value of an asset acquired before that date where the part disposal took place before 6 April 1988;

- if the part sold is small compared with the value of the entire asset or shareholding you can claim to deduct the sale proceeds from the acquisition cost. Where the part disposal is one of land this procedure can be adopted so long as the sale proceeds are both less than £20,000 and one-fifth of the value of the remaining land.

Business assets

If you are in business and dispose of an asset used in your trade you have to pay Capital Gains Tax on the profit of sale. The profit or loss, before taper relief, is calculated in the same way as that on a disposal of an asset you own personally. Where the proceeds of sale are reinvested wholly or partly in other assets for use in the business, payment of the tax on the profit may be wholly or partly postponed by deducting the cost of the replacement assets from the capital gain realized on the disposal of the old asset.

When you come to dispose of your business assets on retirement by sale or gift you may well find that part of the capital gains are either wholly or partly exempt from tax. To qualify automatically for the maximum exemption you must:

CAPITAL GAINS TAX

- Have been in business for at least ten years; and
- Be over age 50 at the time of the disposal.

The same age qualification applies to both sexes. You can only claim this relief before age 50 if you retire prematurely owing to ill health.

'Retirement Relief', as it is known, is being phased out over five years from 1998/99. It ceases to be available from 6 April 2003. The maximum amounts of retirement relief in this transitional period are as follows:

Year	100% relief on gains up to:	50% relief on gains between:
1998–99	£250,000	£250,001–£1,000,000
1999–2000	£200,000	£200,001–£800,000
2000–01	£150,000	£150,001–£600,000
2001–02	£100,000	£100,001–£400,000
2002–03	£50,000	£50,001–£200,000

Ilustration

Ken Vine, who is 62 years old, sold his business in January 2003. He had been trading for well over ten years. The capital gains on the business property and goodwill worked out at £350,000 after taking into account the indexation allowance due. Ken's taxable gain for 2002/03 is £56,250 as follows:

	£	£
Gain		350,000
Less: Retirement relief:		
Full exemption	50,000	
50% exemption (maximum)	75,000	
		125,000
		225,000
Less: Taper relief – 75%		168,750
Taxable gain		£56,250

The following list of assets are those which qualify for the enhanced rate of taper relief applicable to business assets:

* - Assets used in your trade or by a company in which you have a qualifying shareholding.
* - Any of your assets used in your job where you work for a trading employer.

BUSINESS ASSETS

* • All shareholdings held by employees and others in unquoted trading companies.
* • All shareholdings held by employees in quoted trading companies.
* • Shareholdings in a quoted trading company where the holder is not an employee but can exercise at least 5% of the voting rights.
  • Shares owned by employees and office holders of a non-trading company providing the employee does not have a material interest in the company. This is defined as a right to more than 10% of:
    - the profit;
    - the assets on winding up;
    - the voting rights;
    - any class of share capital.

* The qualifying criteria under these headings were relaxed from 6 April 2000.

Where an asset only satisfies the definition of business assets from 6 April 2000 it will be regarded as a non-business asset up to that date. Accordingly the gain will have to be time apportioned so that part will come within the rules for business assets taper relief with the balance as a non-business asset.

Illustration

Patricia Dunne acquired a shareholding in her employer's quoted company in September 1995 for £3,200. Her stake in the company is tiny. She sells the shares in June 2002 realizing £14,500.

The indexation allowance between September 1995 and April 1998 is 0.08.

Until 5 April 2000 the shares were not business assets for taper relief purposes. They did so qualify from 6 April 2000 up to the date of sale. The gain must be apportioned throughout the period of ownership from 6 April 1998.

Patricia's total net chargeable gain for 2002/03 is £5,879 as follows:

	£	£
Sale proceeds of shares		14,500
Less: Cost price	3,200	
Indexation allowance 0.08	256	
		3,456
Gain before taper relief		£11,044

(a) Period as non-business asset

$$\frac{\text{April 1998 to April 2000}}{\text{April 1998 to June 2002}} = \frac{24 \text{ months}}{51 \text{ months}} \times £11,044 = \qquad 5,197$$

Less: Taper relief – 15% (three years plus the bonus year)   780

Chargeable gain   £4,417

(b) Period as business asset

$$\frac{\text{April 2000 to June 2002}}{\text{April 1998 to June 2002}} = \frac{27 \text{ months}}{51 \text{ months}} \times £11,044 = \qquad 5,847$$

Less: Taper relief – 75% (three years)   4,385

Chargeable gain   £1,462

The precise rules which apply in calculating the capital gain on the disposal of a business asset during the course of trading or on retirement are complicated. It is outside the scope of this book to go into them in more detail. You would be well advised to seek professional advice in such circumstances.

Enterprise Investment Scheme

Any gain on the disposal of qualifying shares under the Enterprise Investment Scheme (EIS) is exempt from Capital Gains Tax, providing:

- The Income Tax relief on the investment has not been withdrawn.
- The disposal takes place at least three years after the issue of the shares.

An investor who suffers a loss on disposing of qualifying shares can offset the loss against either:

- Capital Gains in the year the loss is realized; or
- Taxable income in the year of loss or the previous year.

It is also possible for individuals to defer Capital Gains Tax payable on chargeable gains by reinvesting the gains in qualifying EIS shares. For the purposes of deferral relief the chargeable gains must be reinvested within the period beginning one year before, and ending three years after, the original disposal. Deferral relief can be claimed:

- In conjunction with both Income Tax relief (see Chapter 9) and the exemption from Capital Gains Tax (as above) up to the annual investment limit of £150,000; or

- On its own as there is no limit on the amount of gains that can be deferred; or

- In any other combination within the rules chosen by the investor.

Under deferral relief the original liability to Capital Gains Tax crystallizes when the EIS shares are sold.

Venture Capital Trusts

A disposal of shares in a Venture Capital Trust is free of Capital Gains Tax providing:

- The original cost of the shares disposed of did not exceed £100,000 in any one tax year; and

- The company qualifies as a Venture Capital Trust (VCT) both at the time the shares are acquired and also at the date of disposal.

Like the EIS, a further relief is available for individuals who subscribe for new shares in a VCT, as opposed to purchase from a third party. Those individuals can defer a tax charge on a chargeable gain arising on the disposal of any assets, providing:

- The reinvestment in new shares of a VCT is made in a period beginning one year before, and ending one year after, the original disposal; and

- The maximum annual investment limit of £100,000 for Income Tax relief (see Chapter 9) is not breached.

Tax on the deferred gain will be payable when the shares are sold or in other circumstances.

The legislation dealing with both the EIS and VCTs is both lengthy and complex. It contains a number of conditions and restrictions and, as a result, is yet another area of your tax and financial affairs where you would do well to seek professional advice.

Gifts

The capital gain on a gift is calculated by using the market value of the asset at the date of gift. The amount of the gain is reduced by any indexation allowance which is due.

Where the gift is one of business assets you can elect with the

CAPITAL GAINS TAX

transferee for payment of the tax on the gift to be postponed until the asset is subsequently disposed of by the transferee. This same rule also applies in other restricted circumstances. For gifts of some assets where deferral is not available the Capital Gains Tax can be paid in ten equal annual instalments.

Deferred gains on business assets and gifts

Earlier in this chapter you read about the rules for working out the capital gains on assets which you owned at the end of March 1982.
In preceding sections I have made mention of postponing the payment of Capital Gains Tax on gifts and the proceeds of sale of business assets which are reinvested in other assets for use in the business.

Without some special form of relief, the benefit of these rules would be denied where a deferral occurred in the period from 31 March 1982 to 5 April 1988, and a charge to Capital Gains Taxes arises thereafter since the disposal is not of an asset owned on 31 March 1982. The remedy provides for a 50% reduction of the deferred gain.

Illustration

A business asset purchased in 1978 was sold in January 1986. The deferred gain on the sale was £56,000. The replacement asset cost £120,000 and was sold in September 2002 for £180,000. The indexation allowance between January 1986 and April 1998 is 0.689. The chargeable gain is £6,153 as follows:

	£	£
Sale proceeds		180,000
Less: Purchase price	120,000	
Less: Deferred gain	56,000	
	64,000	
Add: 50% of postponed gain	28,000	
	92,000	
Indexation allowance £92,000 × 0.689	63,388	155,388
		24,612
Less: Taper relief – 75%		18,459
2002/03 chargeable gain		£6,153

Inheritances

No Capital Gains Tax is payable on the unrealized profits on your assets at the date of your death. When you inherit an asset you acquire it at the value on the date of death of the deceased. Generally, this rule is also applied whenever you become entitled to assets from a trust.

13

COMPLETING THE RETURN AND CALCULATING YOUR TAX

When you collect your post from the doormat you can always pick out your Tax Return from the other letters. It comes in a distinctive brown envelope at the same time every year. This book is being published around the date when you can expect to receive your Tax Return asking for information about your income and capital gains for the year ended 5 April 2003, as well as the allowances and reliefs you want to claim for the same year. Everybody gets:

- the standard ten-page Return;
- guidance notes;
- supplementary pages based on his or her tax history;
- a tax calculation guide.

The additional colour-coded supplementary pages specific to the income and gains of the taxpayer are:

1. Employment	Pink
2. Share schemes	Purple
3. Self-employment	Orange
4. Partnership	Turquoise
5. Land and property	Red
6. Foreign income and gains and tax credit relief	Mustard
7. Trusts, settlements and the estates of deceased persons	Brown
8. Capital gains	Blue
9. Non-residence	Green

There are no supplementary pages for UK investment income which is entered on the main Return.

When you receive your Return try to avoid the temptation to put it to one side. There is no advantage in delaying. It is better to get started sooner because you will:

- have more time to get help from the Inland Revenue if you need it;
- have more time to save money for any tax you have to pay;
- find out earlier if you are due a tax refund;
- get a big weight off your mind!!

Start by filling in page 2. This tells you which supplementary pages you will need. These can be obtained by telephoning the Orderline on 0845 9000 404 (open 7 days a week from 8 a.m. to 10 p.m). Alternatively you can send a fax to 0845 9000 604. The supplementary pages come with Notes to help you fill in the pages you requested. Help Sheets and leaflets giving more detailed information about particular tax rules for working out the income or capital gains to be declared on the supplementary pages are referrred to in the Notes and are also available from the Orderline.

Then you should decide if you want to calculate your tax or if you want your tax office to do it for you. Remember the deadlines:

30 September 2003

You must send back your completed Tax Return for the year to 5 April 2003 to your tax office by then if you want the Inland Revenue to:

- calculate your tax in time for you to make payment on 31 January 2004; or

- collect tax owing of less than £2,000 through your tax code.

31 January 2004

This date is important for three reasons. By then you must:

- let your tax office have your completed Return;

- pay the balance of any tax you owe for the 2002/03 tax year (unless it is to be collected through your tax code); and

- if appropriate pay your first payment on account for the 2003/04 tax year.

You are now ready to complete the remainder of your Tax Return. Begin by gathering together all the information for the year ended 5 April 2003 on your income, capital gains, reliefs and allowances from the records you have been keeping for the year.

Keeping proper records

For most kinds of income and capital gains you will only need to keep the records given to you by whoever provided that income. This means for those of you

- in employment:

    your Form P60, a certificate your employer will give you after 5 April (the end of the tax year) showing details of pay and tax deducted;

COMPLETING THE RETURN AND CALCULATING YOUR TAX

any Form P45 (part 1A), a certificate from an employer showing details of pay and tax from a job you have left;

any Form P160 (part 1A) you may have been given when you retire and go on to receive a pension paid by your former employer;

your payslips or pay statements;

a note of the amount of any tips or gratuities and details of any other taxable receipts. You are advised to record these as soon as possible after you receive them, not simply estimate them at the end of the year;

Form P11D or P9D or equivalent information from all the employers you have worked for during the year, showing any benefits-in-kind and expenses payments given to you.

- receiving a UK pension or social security benefits:

    your Form P60, a certificate which may be given to you by the payer of your occupational pension, showing the amount of your pension and the tax deducted;

    any other certificate of a pension you received and the tax deducted from it;

    details given to you by The Department of Work and Pensions (DWP) relating to state pensions, taxable state benefits, statutory sick pay, statutory maternity pay and the jobseeker's allowance.

- in business or letting property:

    please refer to Chapter 6 and the section on Records.

- receiving investment income:

    bank and building society statements or passbooks;

    statements of interest and any other income received from your savings and investments; for example, an annuity;

    any tax deduction certificates supplied by your bank or building society;

    dividend vouchers received from UK companies;

    unit trust tax vouchers;

    life insurance chargeable events certificates;

    details of any income you received from a trust.

It is also sensible to keep details of any exceptional amounts — such as an inheritance or other windfall — which you receive and invest.

- making capital gains or losses:

    contracts for the purchase or sale of shares, unit trusts, property or other assets;

    copies of any valuations taken into account in your calculation of capital gains or losses;

    bills, invoices or other evidence of payment records such as bank statements and cheque stubs for costs you claim for the purchase, improvement or sale of assets;

    details of any assets you have given away or put into a trust.

- claiming personal allowances, other deductions or reliefs:

    certificates of interest paid;

    court orders or other legally binding maintenance agreements;

    declarations you have made to charities of gifts under Gift Aid;

    personal pension plan and self-employed premium certificates;

    a birth certificate for any claim where age is relevant;

    a marriage certificate where the married couple's allowance is being claimed;

    notification that you registered as a blind person.

These are some examples of the types of records you would be advised to keep. The list is not exhaustive and does not cover every situation. If you are in any doubt, ask your tax office or Tax Enquiry Centre for advice.

Even if you do not have all the information you need do not let this deter you from preparing your Tax Return and sending it back to your tax office. Of course, you must do all you can to get the information, but if you are unable to provide final figures when the time comes to send off your Tax Return then estimate the missing amounts. Tick box 23.2 on page 9 of your Return and describe in the space provided at 23.5:

- which figures are provisional. You should refer to the appropriate box numbers on your Tax Return or any of the other supplementary pages

COMPLETING THE RETURN AND CALCULATING YOUR TAX

you have completed;

- why you could not give final figures;
- when you expect to be able to provide your tax office with the correct information.

Your tax office will not normally regard a Tax Return as incomplete just because it contains provisional details of income or capital gains provided you have taken all reasonable measures to obtain the final figures, and you make sure that you send them as soon as they are available.

Completing the Return

You must answer all the questions. If you answer 'Yes' you should fill in the boxes which apply to you, otherwise move on to the next question.

Always

- write only in the space provided using blue or black ink;
- only use numbers when you are asked for amounts;
- do not include pence.

There is just not enough space for me to reproduce all the supplementary pages and the core Tax Return in the Guide. I have therefore decided to reproduce the front of the supplementary page on Employment and most of pages 3 to 10 of the Tax Return.

If you have more than one job you will need to fill in a separate copy of the Employment page for each employment. In box 1.8 enter your before-tax salary or wage from your form P60. Put the tax deducted by your employer in box 1.11. The amounts of any benefits-in-kind, which are taxable, will have been worked out by your employer and can be clearly identified from the copy of your form P11D which will be given to you. Enter these benefits and expenses, if appropriate, in boxes 1.12 to 1.23. The reverse of the employment page deals with:

- lump sums and compensation payments;
- foreign earnings;
- expenses you incurred in doing your job;
- repayments of student loans.

COMPLETING THE RETURN

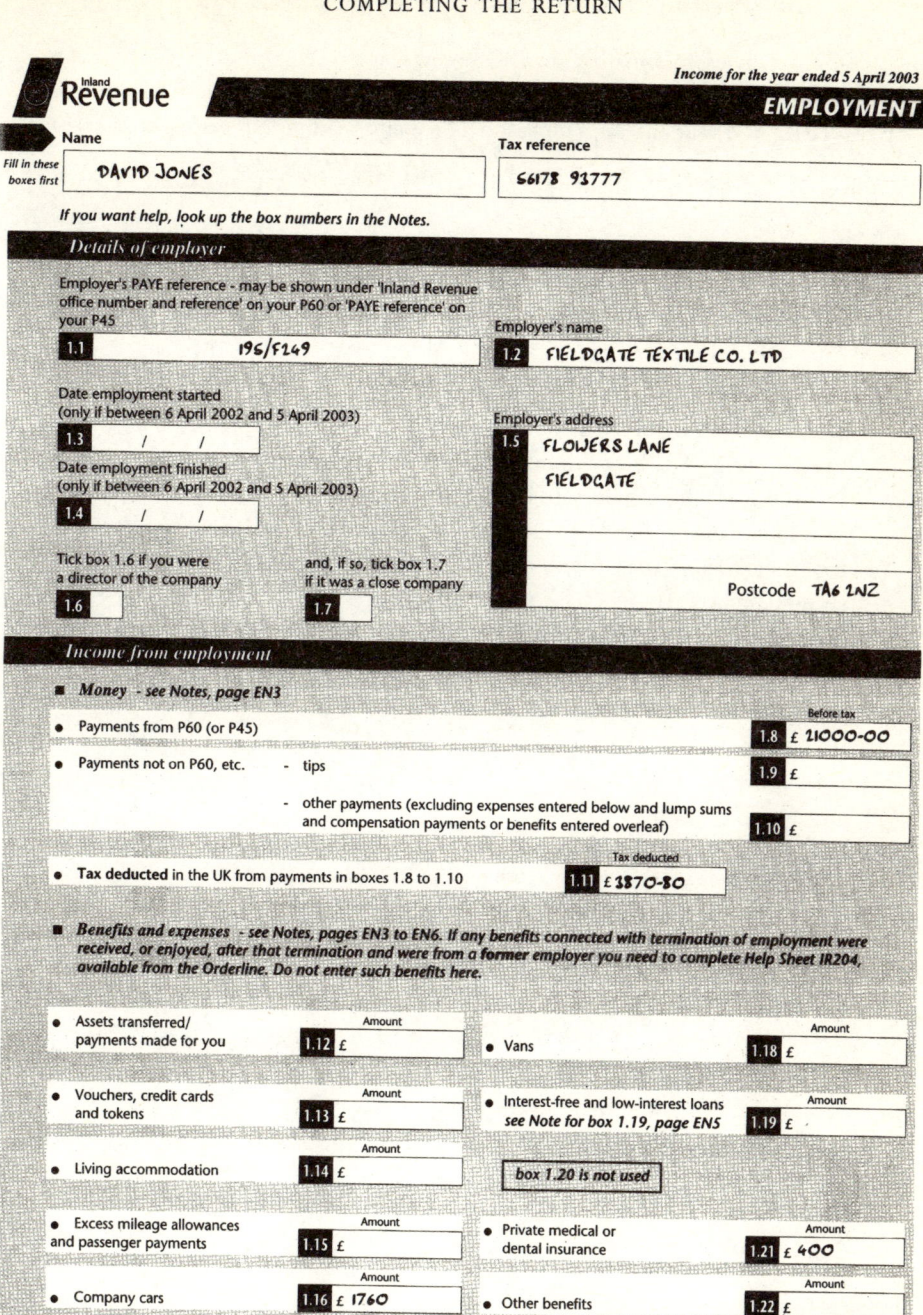

Inland Revenue

Income for the year ended 5 April 2003

EMPLOYMENT

Name
Fill in these boxes first DAVID JONES

Tax reference
56178 93777

If you want help, look up the box numbers in the Notes.

Details of employer

Employer's PAYE reference - may be shown under 'Inland Revenue office number and reference' or on your P60 or 'PAYE reference' on your P45

1.1 196/F249

Employer's name
1.2 FIELDGATE TEXTILE CO. LTD

Date employment started (only if between 6 April 2002 and 5 April 2003)
1.3 / /

Employer's address
1.5 FLOWERS LANE
FIELDGATE

Date employment finished (only if between 6 April 2002 and 5 April 2003)
1.4 / /

Postcode TA6 2NZ

Tick box 1.6 if you were a director of the company
1.6

and, if so, tick box 1.7 if it was a close company
1.7

Income from employment

■ **Money** - *see Notes, page EN3*

- Payments from P60 (or P45)
  Before tax
  1.8 £ 21000-00

- Payments not on P60, etc. - tips
  1.9 £

  - other payments (excluding expenses entered below and lump sums and compensation payments or benefits entered overleaf)
  1.10 £

- **Tax deducted** in the UK from payments in boxes 1.8 to 1.10
  Tax deducted
  1.11 £ 3870-80

■ **Benefits and expenses** - *see Notes, pages EN3 to EN6. If any benefits connected with termination of employment were received, or enjoyed, after that termination and were from a former employer you need to complete Help Sheet IR204, available from the Orderline. Do not enter such benefits here.*

	Amount		Amount
• Assets transferred/ payments made for you	**1.12** £	• Vans	**1.18** £
• Vouchers, credit cards and tokens	**1.13** £	• Interest-free and low-interest loans *see Note for box 1.19, page EN5*	**1.19** £
• Living accommodation	**1.14** £	*box 1.20 is not used*	
• Excess mileage allowances and passenger payments	**1.15** £	• Private medical or dental insurance	**1.21** £ 400
• Company cars	**1.16** £ 1760	• Other benefits	**1.22** £
• Fuel for company cars	**1.17** £ 1930	• Expenses payments received and balancing charges	**1.23** £

BS 12/2002

TAX RETURN ■ EMPLOYMENT: PAGE E1

Please turn over

131

COMPLETING THE RETURN AND CALCULATING YOUR TAX

If you received income from UK savings and investments tick the 'Yes' box at the top of page 3 of your Tax Return. You then need to complete boxes 10.1 to 10.26 as appropriate. The page is divided into two halves:

- Interest

    Take note that there are two boxes 10.1 and 10.8 which specifically deal with interest you have received from UK banks, building societies or National Savings where no tax has been deducted.

- Dividends

    Dividends on your shareholdings come with counterfoils. These show the amount of the dividend and the accompanying tax credit. It is the total of all of your dividends in the year, and tax credits, which should be entered in boxes 10.15 and 10.16. Add these totals together to get the 'dividend/distribution plus credit' figure to be shown in box 10.17. The same procedure should be followed for all other dividends which you have received including those on your unit trust investments and 'scrip' dividends from UK companies. A 'scrip' dividend is where you take up an offer of shares instead of a cash dividend.

COMPLETING THE RETURN

INCOME for the year ended 5 April 2003

Q10 Did you receive any income from UK savings and investments? **YES** ✓

If yes, tick this box and then fill in boxes 10.1 to 10.26 as appropriate. Include only your share from any joint savings and investments.
If not applicable, go to Question 11.

■ Interest

- Interest from UK banks, building societies and deposit takers (interest from UK Internet accounts must be included) - *if you have more than one bank or building society etc. account enter **totals** in the boxes.*

  - enter any bank, building society etc. interest that **has not** had tax taken off. (Most interest is taxed by your bank or building society etc. so make sure you should be filling in box 10.1, rather than boxes 10.2 to 10.4.)

  Taxable amount
  10.1 £

  - enter details of your **taxed** bank or building society etc. interest. *The Working Sheet on page 10 of your Tax Return Guide will help you fill in boxes 10.2 to 10.4.*

Amount after tax deducted	Tax deducted	Gross amount before tax
10.2 £ 272	**10.3** £ 68	**10.4** £ 340

- Interest distributions from UK authorised unit trusts and open-ended investment companies (dividend distributions go below)

Amount after tax deducted	Tax deducted	Gross amount before tax
10.5 £	**10.6** £	**10.7** £

- National Savings & Investments (other than First Option Bonds and Fixed Rate Savings Bonds and the first £70 of interest from an Ordinary Account)

  Taxable amount
  10.8 £ 300

- National Savings & Investments First Option Bonds and Fixed Rate Savings Bonds

Amount after tax deducted	Tax deducted	Gross amount before tax
10.9 £ 144	**10.10** £ 36	**10.11** £ 180

- Other income from UK savings and investments (except dividends)

Amount after tax deducted	Tax deducted	Gross amount before tax
10.12 £	**10.13** £	**10.14** £

■ Dividends

- Dividends and other qualifying distributions from UK companies

Dividend/distribution	Tax credit	Dividend/distribution plus credit
10.15 £ 396	**10.16** £ 44	**10.17** £ 440

- Dividend distributions from UK authorised unit trusts and open-ended investment companies

Dividend/distribution	Tax credit	Dividend/distribution plus credit
10.18 £ 180	**10.19** £ 20	**10.20** £ 200

- Scrip dividends from UK companies

Dividend	Notional tax	Dividend plus notional tax
10.21 £ 36	**10.22** £ 4	**10.23** £ 45

- Non-qualifying distributions and loans written off

Distribution/Loan	Notional tax	Taxable amount
10.24 £	**10.25** £	**10.26** £

BS 12/2002   TAX RETURN: PAGE 3   *Please turn over* ▶

COMPLETING THE RETURN AND CALCULATING YOUR TAX

Did you receive a taxable UK pension, retirement annuity or Social Security benefit in 2002/03? If your pension or benefit is taxable and should be included on the Return tick the 'Yes' box at the top of page 4 and fill in boxes 11.1 to 11.14, as appropriate. As with the Employment page the amount of your pension from a previous employer's pension fund, and the tax deducted throughout the year, will also be shown on a form P60 which has been sent to you. If you are drawing the state pension you should declare the amount of your pension for the 52-week period to 5 April 2003. Particularly where the pension is paid quarterly, there will be a small difference between the income you should declare on the Return and the actual pension received during the tax year. Do not include the £10 Christmas Bonus as this is not taxable.

INCOME for the year ended 5 April 2003, continued

Q11 Did you receive a taxable UK pension, retirement annuity or Social Security benefit?
Read the notes on pages 13 to 15 of the Tax Return Guide.
YES ✓
If yes, tick this box and then fill in boxes 11.1 to 11.14 as appropriate.
If not applicable, go to Question 12.

■ **State pensions and benefits**   Taxable amount for 2002-03

- State Retirement Pension - *enter the total of your entitlements for the year*   **11.1** £ 3926
- Widow's Pension or Bereavement Allowance   **11.2** £
- Widowed Mother's Allowance or Widowed Parent's Allowance   **11.3** £
- Industrial Death Benefit Pension   **11.4** £
- Jobseeker's Allowance   **11.5** £
- Invalid Care Allowance   **11.6** £
- Statutory Sick Pay, Statutory Maternity Pay and Statutory Paternity Pay paid by the Inland Revenue   **11.7** £

                                                                     Tax deducted   Gross amount before tax
- Taxable Incapacity Benefit   **11.8** £   **11.9** £

■ **Other pensions and retirement annuities**

- Pensions (other than State pensions) and retirement annuities - *if you have more than one pension or annuity, please add together and complete boxes 11.10 to 11.12. Provide details of each one in box 11.14*
  Amount after tax deducted   Tax deducted   Gross amount before tax
  11.10 £ 6948-68   **11.11** £ 1051-32   **11.12** £ 8000-00

- Deduction - *see the note for box 11.13 on page 15 of your Tax Return Guide*
  Amount of deduction
  11.13 £

  11.14 FIELDGATE TEXTILE CO. LTD
  FLOWERS LANE
  FIELDGATE
  TA6 2NZ

Question 12 will only be of any concern to you if you received any of the following kinds of income:
- gains on UK life insurance policies, life annuities or capital redemption policies;
- refunds of surplus additional voluntary contributions.

If you do not need to tick the 'Yes' box you can go straight to question 13 which asks you whether you received any other income which has not already been entered elsewhere on your Tax Return. This would include, for example:
- any casual earnings not declared elsewhere;
- accrued income on a transfer of securities;
- income received after your business has ceased.

COMPLETING THE RETURN

Question 14 is the first in the section dealing with reliefs for the year ended 5 April 2003 and is relevant if you want to claim relief for pension contributions. If:

- you pay into both a retirement annuity contract and a personal pension plan; or
- you bring back into 2002/03 payments made after 5 April 2003; or
- you carry back payments in 2002/03 to a previous year; or
- the figure in box 14.5, or 14.9 is more than the appropriate percentage limit of your earnings;

you must telephone the Orderline and ask for Help Sheet IR 330 Pension Payments which includes working sheets to help you complete the boxes.

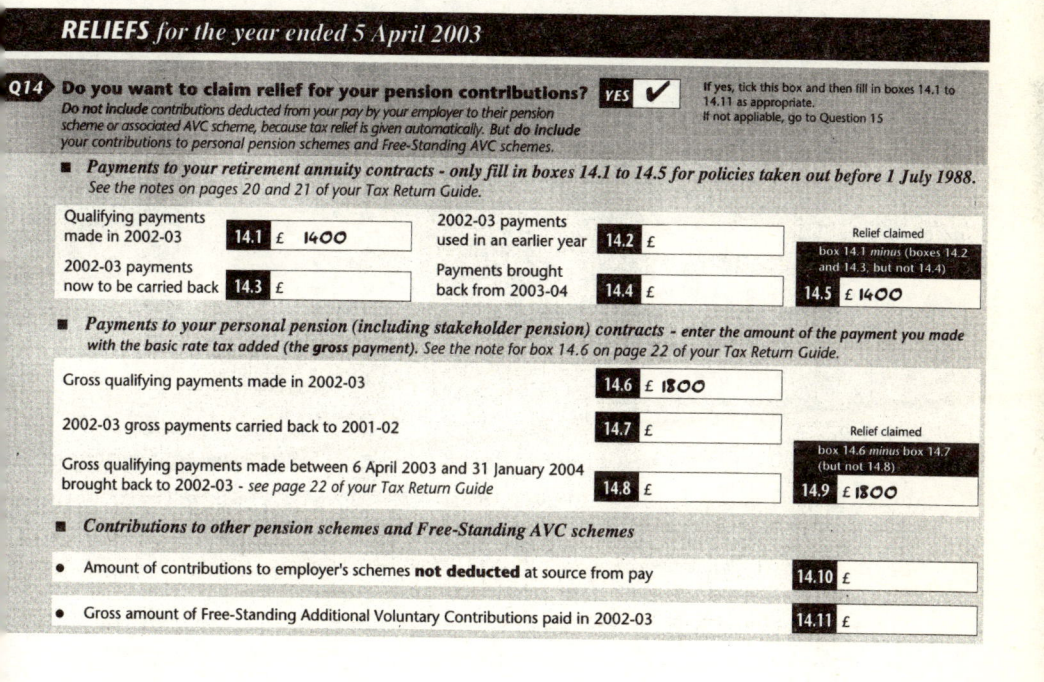

RELIEFS for the year ended 5 April 2003

Q14 Do you want to claim relief for your pension contributions? YES ✓
Do not include contributions deducted from your pay by your employer to their pension scheme or associated AVC scheme, because tax relief is given automatically. But do include your contributions to personal pension schemes and Free-Standing AVC schemes.

If yes, tick this box and then fill in boxes 14.1 to 14.11 as appropriate.
If not appliable, go to Question 15

■ *Payments to your retirement annuity contracts - only fill in boxes 14.1 to 14.5 for policies taken out before 1 July 1988.*
See the notes on pages 20 and 21 of your Tax Return Guide.

| Qualifying payments made in 2002-03 | 14.1 £ 1400 | 2002-03 payments used in an earlier year | 14.2 £ | Relief claimed box 14.1 minus (boxes 14.2 and 14.3, but not 14.4) |
| 2002-03 payments now to be carried back | 14.3 £ | Payments brought back from 2003-04 | 14.4 £ | 14.5 £ 1400 |

■ *Payments to your personal pension (including stakeholder pension) contracts - enter the amount of the payment you made with the basic rate tax added (the **gross** payment). See the note for box 14.6 on page 22 of your Tax Return Guide.*

Gross qualifying payments made in 2002-03 — 14.6 £ 1800

2002-03 gross payments carried back to 2001-02 — 14.7 £

Gross qualifying payments made between 6 April 2003 and 31 January 2004 brought back to 2002-03 - see page 22 of your Tax Return Guide — 14.8 £

Relief claimed box 14.6 minus box 14.7 (but not 14.8)
14.9 £ 1800

■ *Contributions to other pension schemes and Free-Standing AVC schemes*

- Amount of contributions to employer's schemes **not deducted** at source from pay — 14.10 £
- Gross amount of Free-Standing Additional Voluntary Contributions paid in 2002-03 — 14.11 £

Question 15 lists a number of reliefs. Do you want to claim any of them? They include:

- interest paid on qualifying loans;
- maintenance or alimony payments you are making;
- your subscriptions for new ordinary shares in a Venture Capital Trust;
- subscriptions under the Enterprise Investment Scheme;
- payments to a trade union or friendly society for death benefits.

COMPLETING THE RETURN AND CALCULATING YOUR TAX

Q15 Do you want to claim any of the following reliefs?
If you have made any annual payments, after basic rate tax, answer 'Yes' to Question 15 and fill in box 15.9. If you have made any gifts to charity go to Question 15A

YES ✓ — If yes, tick this box and then fill in boxes 15.1 to 15.12, as appropriate. If not applicable, go to Question 15A

- Interest eligible for relief on qualifying loans — **15.1** £ 860 *(Amount of payment)*
- Maintenance or alimony payments you have made under a court order, Child Support Agency assessment or legally binding order or agreement — **15.2** £ 1780 *(Amount claimed up to £2,110)*

  To claim this relief, either you or your former spouse must have been 65 or over on 5 April 2000. So, if **your** date of birth, which is entered in box 22.6, is after 5 April 1935 then you must enter your former **spouse's** date of birth in box 15.2A — *see pages 23 and 24 of your Tax Return Guide*

  15.2A 11 / 10 / 30 *(Former spouse's date of birth)*

- Subscriptions for Venture Capital Trust shares (up to £100,000) — **15.3** £ 8000 *(Amount on which relief is claimed)*
- Subscriptions under the Enterprise Investment Scheme (up to £150,000) - *also provide details in box 23.5, see page 24 of your Tax Return Guide* — **15.4** £ *(Amount on which relief is claimed)*
- Community Investment Tax relief - invested amount relating to previous tax year(s) and on which relief is due — **15.5** £
- Community Investment Tax relief - invested amount for current tax year — **15.6** £ — **15.7** £ *(Total amount on which relief is claimed box 15.5 + box 15.6)*
- Post-cessation expenses, pre-incorporation losses brought forward and losses on relevant discounted securities, etc. - *see pages 24 and 25 of your Tax Return Guide* — **15.8** £ *(Amount of payment)*
- Annuities and annual payments — **15.9** £ *(Payments made)*
- Payments to a trade union or friendly society for death benefits — **15.10** £ *(Half amount of payment)*
- Payment to your employer's compulsory widow's, widower's or orphan's benefit scheme - *available in some circumstances – first read the notes on page 25 of your Tax Return Guide* — **15.11** £ *(Relief claimed)*
- Relief claimed on a qualifying distribution on the **redemption** of bonus shares or securities. — **15.12** £ *(Relief claimed)*

You may be entitled to higher-rate tax relief on donations to charities under Gift Aid. Such payments are regarded as having been made by you after tax at the basic rate has been deducted. No further tax relief is due unless you pay tax the the top rate of 40%.

You should enter in boxes 15A.1, 15A.2 and 15A.3 (as appropriate) the amount of any payments made by you in the year to 5 April 2003, even if you are not claiming higher-rate tax relief. Cash gifts to Community Amateur Sports Clubs, using Gift Aid, are treated in the same way as Gift Aid payments to charity.

Perhaps by the time you complete your Tax Return and send it back to your Tax Office you have made Gift Aid donations in the 2003/04 tax year starting on 6 April 2003. You can elect to have those payments treated as though they were made in the year to 5 April 2003.

COMPLETING THE RETURN

ALLOWANCES *for the year ended 5 April 2003*

Q15A **Do you want to claim relief on gifts to charity?** **YES** ✓
If you have made any Gift Aid payments answer 'Yes' to Question 15A. You should include Gift Aid payments to Community Amateur Sports Clubs here. You can elect to include in this Return Gift Aid payments made between 6 April 2003 and the date you send in this Return. See page 26 in the Tax Return Guide and the leaflet enclosed on Gift Aid.

If yes, tick this box and then read page 26 of your Tax Return Guide. Fill in boxes 15A.1 to 15A.5 as appropriate. If not applicable, go to Question 16.

- Gift Aid and payments under charitable covenants made between 6 April 2002 and 5 April 2003 — **15A.1** £ 1,200
- Enter in box 15A.2 the total of any 'one off' payments included in box 15A.1 — **15A.2** £ 1,000
- Enter in box 15A.3 the amount of Gift Aid payments made after 5 April 2003 but treated as if made in the tax year 2002-03 — **15A.3** £ 400
- Gifts of qualifying investments to charities – shares and securities — **15A.4** £ 2,500
- Gifts of qualifying investments to charities – real property — **15A.5** £

Most of pages 6 and 7, and indeed question 16, are devoted to the allowances for the year ended 5 April 2003 which you may want to claim. There are separate sections covering all the personal allowances and the individuals – whether they be single, married, or elderly – who can claim them. In each case there is a space for you to enter the information the Inland Revenue need to make sure you are given the full and right tax allowances.

The first part of this section is for you to make a claim for the special blind person's allowance. You will need to give the name of the local authority, or equivalent body, with whom you have registered your blindness as well as the date of registration.

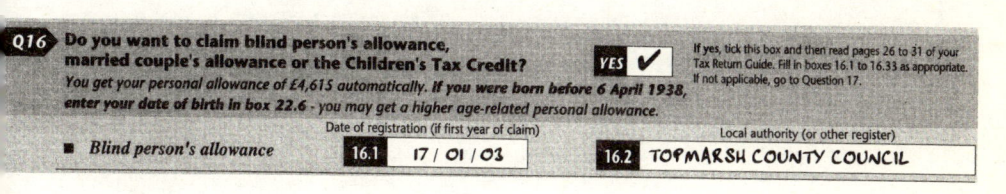

Q16 **Do you want to claim blind person's allowance, married couple's allowance or the Children's Tax Credit?** **YES** ✓
You get your personal allowance of £4,615 automatically. If you were born before 6 April 1938, enter your date of birth in box 22.6 – you may get a higher age-related personal allowance.

If yes, tick this box and then read pages 26 to 31 of your Tax Return Guide. Fill in boxes 16.1 to 16.33 as appropriate. If not applicable, go to Question 17.

■ Blind person's allowance — Date of registration (if first year of claim) **16.1** 17/01/03 — Local authority (or other register) **16.2** TOPMARSH COUNTY COUNCIL

Then comes the section on claiming the married couple's allowance. This can only be claimed if either you, or your husband or wife, were born before 6 April 1935. So you can only claim the allowance in 2002/03 if either of you had reached 65 years of age before 6 April 2000.

It is only necessary for a married woman to fill in Boxes 16.10 to 16.13 where she and her husband have agreed that either half, or all, the married couple's allowance be allocated to her.

COMPLETING THE RETURN AND CALCULATING YOUR TAX

■ **Married couple's allowance** – In 2002-03 married couple's allowance can only be claimed if either you, or your husband or wife, were born **before 6 April 1935**. So you can only claim the allowance in 2002-03 if either of you had reached 65 years of age before 6 April 2000. Further guidance is given beginning on page 27 of your Tax Return Guide.

If **both** you and your husband or wife were born after 5 April 1935 you cannot claim; **do not** complete boxes 16.3 to 16.13.

If **you can claim** fill in boxes 16.3 and 16.4 if you are a married man or if you are a married woman and you are claiming half or all of the married couple's allowance.

- Enter your date of birth (if born before 6 April 1935)   **16.3** 12 / 02 / 33
- Enter your spouse's date of birth (if born before 6 April 1935 **and** if older than you)   **16.4** 26 / 09 / 20

Then, if you are a married man fill in boxes 16.5 to 16.9. If you are a married woman fill in boxes 16.10 to 16.13.

- Wife's full name   **16.5** WENDY MARTIN   Date of marriage (if after 5 April 2002)   **16.6** / /

                                                   Half   All

- Tick box 16.7, or box 16.8, if you or your wife have allocated half, or all, of the minimum amount of the allowance to her   **16.7** ✓   **16.8**

- Enter in box 16.9 the date of birth of any previous wife with whom you lived at any time during 2002-03. Read *'Special rules if you are a man who married in the year ended 5 April 2003'* on page 28 before completing box 16.9.   **16.9** / /

                                                   Half   All

- Tick box 16.10, or box 16.11, if you or your husband have allocated half, or all, of the minimum amount of the allowance to you   **16.10**   **16.11**

- Husband's full name   **16.12**   Date of marriage (if after 5 April 2002)   **16.13** / /

The remaining part of page 6, and most of page 7, is taken up with the claim you can make for the Children's Tax Credit. Before completing the claim I recommend you look back to the section in Chapter 2 on the Credit and also read pages 28 to 31 of your Tax Return Guide.

■ **Children's Tax Credit** – even if you have already completed a separate Children's Tax Credit (CTC) claim form and received the relief in your tax code, you should still fill in boxes 16.14 to 16.26, as directed. Any reference to 'partner' in this question means the person you lived with during the year to 5 April 2003 – your husband or wife, or someone you lived with as husband or wife.

Guidance for claiming CTC is on pages 28 to 31 of your Tax Return Guide. Please read the notes before completing your claim, particularly if either you, or your partner, were liable to tax above the basic rate in the year to 5 April 2003.

- Enter in box 16.14 the date of birth of a child living with you who was born on or after 6 April 1986. If you have a child living with you who was born on or after 6 April 2002 make sure you enter their date of birth in this box in preference to claiming for an older child.   **16.14** 10 / 12 / 90

- Tick box 16.15 if the child was your own child or one you looked after at your own expense. If not, you cannot claim CTC – go to box 16.27, if appropriate, or Question 17.   **16.15** ✓

- Tick box 16.16 if the child lived with you **throughout** the year to 5 April 2003.   **16.16** ✓
  If you ticked box 16.16 and
  - you were a lone or single claimant, you have finished this question; go to Question 17,
  - you have a partner, go to box 16.18.

- If the child lived with you for only **part of the year** you may only be entitled to a proportion of the CTC. Enter in box 16.17 your share in £s that **you have agreed** with any other claimants that you may claim for this child. But leave boxes 16.17 to 16.25 blank if you separated from, or started living with, your partner during the year to 5 April 2003. Special rules apply to work out your entitlement; ask the Orderline for *Help Sheet IR343: Claiming Children's Tax Credit when your circumstances change* which explains how to complete box 16.26.   **16.17** £

COMPLETING THE RETURN

ALLOWANCES *for the year ended 5 April 2003, continued*

■ **Children's Tax Credit**, *continued*

If you lived with your partner (for CTC this means your husband or wife, or someone you lived with as husband and wife) for the whole of the year to 5 April 2003, fill in boxes 16.18 to 16.25 as appropriate.

- Enter in box 16.18 your partner's surname **16.18 SONIA KENDALL**
- Enter in box 16.19 your partner's National Insurance number **16.19 D F 2 1 8 2 1 9 8**
- Tick
  - box 16.20 if you had the higher income in the year to 5 April 2003, **16.20**
  or
  - box 16.21 if your partner had the higher income in that year **16.21**
- Tick box 16.22 if either of you were chargeable to tax above the basic rate limit in the year to 5 April 2003. **16.22**

If you ticked boxes 16.20 and 16.22 your entitlement will be reduced – see page 30 of your Tax Return Guide; your partner cannot claim CTC - go to box 16.28, or Question 17 as appropriate.

If you ticked boxes 16.21 and 16.22 your partner's entitlement will be reduced; you cannot claim CTC – go to box 16.27, or Question 17, as appropriate.

If neither of you were chargeable above the basic rate and you had the lower income and
- *you don't want to claim half of the entitlement to CTC, and*
- *you didn't make an election for CTC to go to the partner with the lower income*

you have finished this part of your Return - go to boxes 16.27 or 16.28, or Question 17, as appropriate (your partner should claim CTC if they have not already done so).

Otherwise, tick one of boxes 16.23 to 16.25
- I had the higher income and I am claiming all of our entitlement to CTC **16.23 ✓**
- We are both making separate claims for half of our entitlement to CTC **16.24**
- We elected before 6 April 2002, or because of our special circumstances, during the year to 5 April 2003 (see page 31 of your Tax Return Guide), for the partner with the lower income to claim all of our entitlement to CTC **16.25**
- If you separated from, or starting living with, your partner in the year to 5 April 2003, enter in box 16.26 the amount of CTC you are claiming *(following the guidance in Help Sheet IR343: Claiming Children's Tax Credit when your circumstances change.)* **16.26 £**

Finally on page 7 is a section about transferring surplus allowances.

The last three pages of the Return ask for other information for the year ended 5 April 2003 and are all relatively straightforward. When the Return is finished it must be signed and dated in the space provided on page 10. Bear in mind the wording of the declaration: 'The information I have given in this Tax Return is correct and complete to the best of my knowledge and belief'. Then send the form back to your tax office. As there is no space in each section of the Return you may well need to prepare separate statements of, for example, your interest and dividend income in order to arrive at the single figures which need to be entered on the Return. I strongly recommend that copies of any supporting statements or schedules which you prepare should be sent to your tax office along with the Return. Do not, however, send in any building society statements, dividend vouchers and other financial records. Just keep them safely.

If, after you have sent off your Tax Return, you find that you have made a mistake, let your tax office know at once so that it can be taken into account.

COMPLETING THE RETURN AND CALCULATING YOUR TAX

Calculating your tax

You should receive a Tax Calculation Guide with your Tax Return. This will help you if you want to calculate your tax. If your tax affairs are more complicated you will need to ask for the Comprehensive Tax Calculation Guide. Alternatively, you may want to consider using the Inland Revenue's Internet service for Self-Assessment (if so, go to www.inlandrevenue.gov.uk). The key steps in calculating your tax bill are as follows:

- bring together all the non-savings income you have entered on your Return;
- total the deductions and allowances you have claimed for the year;
- add your savings and dividend income to arrive at your total income, take away your deductions and allowances to get your taxable income, then work out the tax due, so far;
- take off further allowances, deductions and tax paid at source – then work out your total Income Tax, Class 4 National Insurance Contributions (if you are self-employed or in partnership) and any Student Loan Repayments – to give you the figure to enter in box 18.3 on page 8 of your Return;
- work out what you have to pay for 2002/03 by 31 January 2004;
- calculate any 2003/04 payments on account you may have to make on 31 January and 31 July 2004.

Illustration

George Salmon is employed by a local company as a senior engineer. Since the beginning of July 1996 he has regularly been asked to speak at seminars and write articles for trade magazines. George is 53 (he was born on 8 February 1950) and is happily married to Lynne. They do not have any children. He owns a modest number of investments and his spare cash is deposited in National Savings and building society accounts.

George files his Tax Return for the year to 5 April 2003 on 23 October 2003. It shows the following entries:

CALCULATING YOUR TAX

	£	Box Number in Return
(1) Employment		
Salary	36,500.00	1.8
Tax deducted by employer	9,721.60	1.11
Subscription to the Association of Mechanical Engineers	100.00	1.34
Company car benefit	3,700.00	1.16
Fuel benefit for company car	2,850.00	1.17

	£	Box Number in Return
(2) Self-Employment		
Adjusted profit shown by the accounts for the year to 30 June 2002	10,000.00	3.92
George applied for, and was granted, permission to defer payment of Class 4 National Insurance Contributions		
Tax payments of £1,200 have been made on both 31 January 2003 and 31 July 2003 based on George's tax liability for 2001/02		
Personal pension premiums paid in 2002/03 (based on self-employed earnings and paid gross)	2,500.00	14.9
(3) Savings Income		
National Savings Income Bonds (paid gross)	250.00	10.8
Building Society interest received		
– gross interest	600.00	10.4
tax deducted	120.00	10.3
net interest	480.00	10.2
Dividends from share investments		
– gross	1,500.00	10.17
tax credit	150.00	10.16
dividends	1,350.00	10.15

(4) Reliefs

In the year George paid £312 (equivalent to £400 before tax) under Gift Aid to the Cancer Research Campaign   15A.1

Unfortunately, the Inland Revenue's Tax Calculation Guide runs to a minimum of 17 pages and there is insufficient space to reproduce them here. An abbreviated version of George Salmon's tax calculation is as follows:

	£	£
Employment		
Salary and taxable benefits	43,050	
Less: Professional subscription	100	
		42,950
Self employment		10,000
UK interest (before tax)		
Interest from UK Building Society	600	
National Savings interest paid gross	250	
		850
UK dividends and tax credits		1,500
Total income		**55,300**
Deductions for:		
Self employed contributions to personal pension plans		2,500
Gift Aid payment		400
Total deductions		**2,900**
Total income less deductions		52,400
Allowances given as deduction from income:		
Personal allowance		4,615
Net Income Chargeable to Tax		47,785

142

Tax thereon:

Non-savings income at starting rate, £1,920 at 10%	192.00
Non-savings income at basic rate, £27,980 at 22%	6,155.60
Non-savings income at higher rate, £15,535 at 40%	6,214.00
Savings (excluding dividends) at higher savings rate, £850 at 40%	340.00
Dividends at higher dividend rate, £1,500 at 32.5%	487.50

Carried forward	13,389.10
Brought forward	13,389.10

Allowances and reliefs given in terms of tax:

Non-repayable tax credits on dividends	(150.00)
Income tax due after allowances and reliefs	**13,239.10**
Recoverable tax on Gift Aid payment	88.00
Income tax	**13,327.10**

Tax paid at source:

On salary	(9,721.60)
On UK savings	(120.00)
Income Tax due for 2002/03	**3,485.50**

TAX PAYMENTS

Tax due for 2002/03 (as above)	3,485.50
Payment on account made 31 January 2003	(1,200.00)
Payment on account made 31 July 2003	(1,200.00)
Balance due for 2002/03	**1,085.50**
Add: First payment on account for 2003/04	1,742.75
Amount due on 31 January 2004	**2,828.25**
Second payment on account for 2003/04	1,742.75
Amount due on 31 July 2004	**1,742.75**

COMPLETING THE RETURN AND CALCULATING YOUR TAX

From his tax calculation George will then be able to fill in question 18 of his Tax Return as follows:

OTHER INFORMATION *for the year ended 5 April 2003, continued*

Q18 Do you want to calculate your tax and, if appropriate, any Student Loan Repayment? YES ✓

Use your Tax Calculation Guide then fill in boxes 18.1 to 18.8 as appropriate.

- Unpaid tax for earlier years **included in your tax code for 2002-03** — 18.1 £
- Tax due for 2002-03 included in your tax code for a later year — 18.2 £
- Student Loan Repayment due — 18.2A £
- Total tax, Class 4 NIC and Student Loan Repayment due for 2002-03 **before** you made any payments on account *(put the amount in brackets if an overpayment)* — 18.3 £ 3485-50
- Tax due for earlier years — 18.4 £
- Tax overpaid for earlier years — 18.5 £
- Tick box 18.6 if you are claiming to reduce your 2003-04 payments on account. Make sure you enter the **reduced** amount of your first payment in box 18.7. Then, in the 'Additional information' box, box 23.5 on page 9, say why you are making a claim — 18.6
- Your first payment on account for 2003-04 *(include the pence)* — 18.7 £ 1742-75
- Any 2003-04 tax you are reclaiming now — 18.8 £

What the Inland Revenue does

When your completed Tax Return is received by your tax office it will be processed as quickly as possible based on your figures, to sort out how much tax you owe, or how much tax is due back to you from the Inland Revenue. Any simple mistakes will be corrected right away and you will be told about them. This may simply be because your figures do not add up.

You will be sent a calculation of your tax position if you have asked the Inland Revenue to do it for you. If you have worked out your own tax bill, and it is wrong, you will also be advised of the mistakes you have made.

Once your Tax Return has been processed it will be checked. The Inland Revenue have 12 months from 31 January 2004 to check your Tax Return for the year ended 5 April 2003 (longer if you are late in submitting your Return). Remember that enquiries may be made into your figures and you may be asked by your tax office to send in your records in support of them.

14

TAX PAYMENTS, INTEREST, SURCHARGES AND PENALTIES

Two further features of Self-Assessment are:

- one set of payment dates for tax not paid at source;
- a clear statement of your 'account' with the Inland Revenue, showing tax payments both made and due.

Tax payments

Taxpayers with tax to pay on their Self-Assessment must pay the tax due by 31 January following the end of the tax year covered by the Return. The one exception to this rule deals with employees or pensioners who submit their Returns to their tax office by 30 September following the end of the tax year. If the tax they owe is less than £2,000 they can opt to have it collected through the PAYE system.

Illustration

Jean Wilkinson sends her 2002/03 Tax Return to her tax office on 26 June 2003. The Inland Revenue calculate she owes tax of £380 for the year. She decides to pay the amount due through the PAYE system. The allowances in her notice of coding for 2004/05 will be restricted to collect the liability month by month throughout the year.

Some taxpayers – mainly the self-employed – will also make two payments on account for the tax year before the Return for that year needs to be submitted. These payments on account are due on:

- 31 January in the tax year; and
- 31 July following the end of the tax year.

If you work out your own tax you will also calculate your own payments on account. Normally you will split into two equal parts the tax paid in the previous tax year (after taking off tax paid at source and any Capital Gains Tax) and pay one half on 31 January and the second instalment six months later at the end of July. However, if you ask your tax office to work out your tax then they will also let you know if you have to make payments on account, and for how much.

You will not need to make payments on account:

- if your liability to Income Tax and Class 4 National Insurance Contributions for the previous tax year – after deducting tax suffered at source on, for example, dividends and Building Society interest – is less than £500; or

- if more than 80% of your liability to Income Tax and Class 4 National Insurance Contributions for the previous tax year was satisfied by tax paid at source;
- for Capital Gains Tax.

These tests mean that most employees and pensioners who complete Returns will not have to make payments on account under Self-Assessment.

Perhaps, because of a change in your circumstances, the calculation of your payments on account for the year (based, of course, on your tax liability for the previous year) seems likely to overstate your liability for the year.

This might happen if you expect:

- Your income in 2003/04 to be lower than your income in 2002/03.
- Your allowances or reliefs to be higher.
- That more of your income will be taxed at source in 2003/04, because:
  - It will be taxed under PAYE; or
  - More of your income will come from savings, for example, interest on bank or building society deposits taxed at source.

You can then claim to reduce your payments on account. This should be done by using form SA303 which is available from any tax office. The form also gives you guidance on how to fill it in. When completed, send it back to your tax office.

If your claim to reduce your payments on account subsequently turns out to be excessive then you will be asked to pay interest on the difference between the tax actually paid to the Collector of Taxes and the amounts that should have been paid.

The tax payment dates for 2002/03 are:

	Due date for Tax Payments on Account	Due date for Final Balance
Rental income and untaxed investment income	50% 31/01/2003 50% 31/07/2003	31/01/2004
Business profits		
Underpaid PAYE (where not coded)		
Higher Rate Tax on investment income (taxed at source)		
Capital Gains Tax	N/A	31/01/2004

Statements of Account

Under Self-Assessment, taxpayers get statements showing their account with the Inland Revenue, the main features of which are:

- the total tax payable is shown near the top of the statement, below the address. If no tax is due this will also be shown;
- the statement includes a final total line so that it is possible to work through the detailed entries and reconcile these with the total tax payable;
- in most instances the amount payable will be printed on the accompanying payslip.

If you are making payments on account you can expect to receive the following statements up to February 2004:

July 2003	To remind you of the second payment on account for 2002/03 due on 31 July.
August 2003	To tell you of any outstanding balance of the second payment on account. The statement will also include an amount for interest due to date.
January 2004	To advise you of your balancing payment for 2002/03 and your first payment on account for 2003/04, both due on 31 January 2004.
February 2004	To show any outstanding amounts of your Self-Assessment for 2002/03 and your first payment on account for 2003/04. The statement will also include a charge for interest due to date.

Taxpayers who do not need to make payments on account will not, of course, receive so many statements of account from their tax office. If you are late in paying your tax you will receive additional statements each month.

Paying your tax

If you pay your tax by post, send the payslip and your cheque, both unfolded, in the envelope provided to your Accounts Office. The Inland Revenue requests that you do not please staple or attach paperclips to cheques. You can help your Accounts Office deal promptly with a payment from you by:

- including a separate letter if you are sending a post-dated cheque, or want to give further information about your payment;
- paying on time – you will then avoid incurring interest charges.

But do not send cash through the post

You can also pay by one of the other following methods:
- internet or telephone banking;
- bank giro;
- at a post office;
- Girobank;
- debit card (Switch, Solo or Visa Delta) by calling 0845 305 1000 and quoting your Unique Taxpayer Reference.

You can provide for the payment of a future tax liability by purchasing a certificate of tax deposit. Certificates can be bought from the Collector of Taxes. They earn interest from the date of purchase up until the normal due date for payment of the liability. The interest is taxable.

Date of payment

The effective times of receipt of tax are as follows:

Payment Method	Effective Date of Payment
Handed in at Inland Revenue office or received by post (except below)	day of receipt by the Inland Revenue
Received by post following a day when the office has been closed for whatever reason (including a weekend)	the day the office was first closed (for payments received on Monday, the effective date will be the previous Saturday)
Electronic Funds Transfer (EFT) – payment by BACS or CHAPS (Clearing House Automated Payment System)	one working day immediately before the date that the value is received. (A working day is defined as a Bank of England working day.)
Bank Giro or Girobank	three working days prior to the date of processing by the Inland Revenue

Interest

If you delay paying your tax you will be charged interest. This applies to both payments on account and balancing payments. The rate of interest is worked out on a set formula. It is an average of the base rates of six main banks (rounded to the nearest whole number) plus 2.5%. At the time of going into print the rate is 6.5%. The interest is calculated from the due date up until payment. You cannot claim tax relief on the interest.

You need to be aware of the circumstances when the imposition of interest would clearly be unfair and can be justifiably contested. The Inland Revenue Code of Practice entitled 'Mistakes by the Inland Revenue' suggests that an Inspector will waive interest if delays have occurred for more than six months over and above the 28-day target of dealing with such matters. The booklet goes on:

'If there is no good reason for a delay, and we have taken more than six months in total – over and above the twenty-eight day target we have set ourselves we will, for amounts unpaid, or not repaid, because of our delay:

- Give up interest that arose on unpaid tax during the period of our delay; or
- Pay you interest (called 'repayment interest') on money we owed you during the period of our delay; and
- Pay any reasonable costs which you have incurred as a direct result of our delay.'

You will be paid interest on any overpayments of the following:

- payments on account of Income Tax;
- Income Tax and Capital Gains Tax paid;
- surcharges on late payment of tax;
- any penalties imposed.

The interest, called repayment supplement, is not taxable. The rate of interest is worked out by first of all taking 1% off the average base rate mentioned above. The resulting figure is then further reduced by the 20% rate of Income Tax deducted at source from savings income. At the time of going into print the rate of repayment supplement is 2.5%.

Remission of tax

Collection of arrears of Income Tax or Capital Gains Tax may be waived if the arrears result from the Inland Revenue's failure to make proper and timely use of information supplied by:

- the taxpayer about his or her own income, capital gains or personal circumstances;
- an employer, where the information affects an employee's notice of coding; or
- the DWP about a taxpayer's retirement, disability or widow's State Pension.

The concession is normally only given where the taxpayer:

- could reasonably have believed that his or her tax affairs were in order; and
- is notified of the arrears by the end of the tax year following that in which it arose.

Surcharges

With Self-Assessment come surcharges. They will be levied automatically on late payment of Capital Gains Tax or the final amount of Income Tax owing as follows:

Tax unpaid by 28 February 5% of unpaid tax
(one month after the tax was due)

Tax unpaid by 31 July Further 5% of tax unpaid
(six months after the tax was due)

Notice of any surcharge must be served on you formally by the Inland Revenue. You do have the right to appeal within 30 days if you think you have a reasonable excuse. You might be successful with your appeal if there is clear evidence that your cheque was lost in the post or in the event of serious illness. Lack of funds, apart from exceptional circumstances, or cheques wrongly made out are examples of cases when your appeal would be rejected.

The Inland Revenue booklet SA/BK5 contains examples of what the Inland Revenue will regard as a reasonable excuse for appealing against a surcharge for the late payment of tax.

Penalties

The main penalties under Self-Assessment are:

Offence	Penalty
You do not submit your Tax Return to your Tax Office by 31 January after the end of the tax year	£100
Your Return is still outstanding after a further six months	Further £100

The above penalties are automatic but will be reduced if the tax owing is less. Up to £60 per day in further penalties can be levied on application to the Commissioners by the Inland Revenue.

If taxpayers have a genuinely good excuse for missing the annual 31 January deadline for submitting Tax Returns, they can appeal against the automatic £100 late filing penalty.

Examples of what may be accepted by the Inland Revenue as a reasonable excuse include:

- Where the Tax Return was not received by the taxpayer.

- Where the Tax Return was lost in the post or delayed because of:
  - fire or flood at the Post Office where the Tax Return was handled;
  - prolonged industrial action within the Post Office;
  - an unforeseen event which disrupted the postal services;
- Where a taxpayer lost his or her tax records as a result of fire, flood or theft.
- Serious illness.
- Death of a spouse, domestic partner or close relative.

Examples of what the Inland Revenue will not agree as a reasonable excuse include:

- Tax Return too difficult.
- Pressure of work.
- Lack of information.
- Absence of reminders from the Inland Revenue.

Returns still outstanding after the anniversary of the filing date	£200 and a further sum up to the amount of the tax payable
You don't receive a Tax Return and fail to notify the Inland Revenue of chargeability to tax within six months of the end of the tax year	Not exceeding the tax due
Fraudulently or negligently delivering an incorrect Tax Return	Up to the amount of the difference between the tax actually payable and that which was shown as due
Not notifying the Inland Revenue that you have started up in business within 3 months after the end of the month in which you commenced your self-employment	£100
Failure to produce documents during an Inland Revenue enquiry	An initial penalty of £50 followed by a further penalty of up to £30 for each day during which the failure continues
Failure to maintain and keep records	Up to £3,000
Fraudulently or negligently claiming to reduce interim tax payments	Up to an amount equivalent to the difference between the tax paid and the tax that should have been paid

Generally a penalty determination must be made, or proceedings commenced, within six years of the date on which the penalty was incurred. The rules allow for this to be extended to any later time within three years of the final determination of the tax liability.

15

ELECTIONS AND CLAIMS – TIME LIMITS

You will already have gathered that certain options available to you as a taxpayer are dependent on you submitting an election or claim to the appropriate authority. As these will usually involve a saving in tax it is important to appreciate that you often need to act within prescribed time limits. This chapter brings together those elections and claims which are most likely to concern you. It also sets out the time available during which they must be submitted to the Inspector of Taxes or Customs and Excise. It is by no means exhaustive.

Election/Claim	Time Limit
Chapter 2 – Personal Allowances and Tax Credits	
The various elections for the transfer of the married couple's and blind person's allowances	Generally before the start of the tax year for which it is to have effect
Claim to the personal allowances detailed in the chapter	No later than five years after 31 January next following the end of the tax year
Transfer of excess allowances between husband and wife	No later than five years after 31 January next following the end of the tax year
Transfer of Children's Tax Credit	Generally before the start of the tax year for which it is to have effect
Chapter 5 – Value Added Tax	
Application for Registration	No later than 30 days from the end of the month after the one when turnover exceeds the registration limit
Submission to Customs and Excise of each VAT Return with full payment of the tax due	Within one month after the end of the VAT accounting period
Claim for Bad Debt Relief	When a debt remains unpaid for more than six months
Chapter 6 – The Self-Employed	
Relief for post-cessation expenses	No later than one year after 31 January next following the tax year in which the payments are made

Creating a separate pool to work out the capital allowances on an asset with a short life expectancy	No later than one year after 31 January next following the tax year in which the period of account ended in which the expenditure is incurred
Relief for the loss sustained in the tax year against other income of the same year or the preceding year	Within one year after 31 January next following the tax year in which the loss arose
Relief for a trading loss against the profits arising from the same trade in subsequent periods	Within five years after 31 January next following the tax year in which the loss was sustained
Relief for the loss in the first four years of assessment of a new business to be given against the income of the three preceding years of assessment	No later than one year after 31 January next following the tax year in which the loss occurred
Relief for trading losses to be offset against Capital Gains	No later than one year after 31 January next following the tax year
Relief for the loss in the last 12 months of trading to be given against the profits of the same trade which were assessed in the three tax years prior to the year in which the trade was discontinued	Within five years after 31 January next following the tax year in which the trade ceased

Chapter 8 – Personal Pensions

Personal and stakeholder pension contributions to be treated as paid in the preceding year of assessment	The contributions must be paid by 31 January following the end of the tax year. The claim must be made when, or before, the premium is paid
Retirement annuity premiums to be treated as paid in the preceding year of assessment	By 31 January after the tax year in which payment was made

Chapter 9 – Investment Income

An election to opt out of the Rent-a-Room relief for a particular tax year, or withdrawal of an election	Within one year after 31 January next following the tax year

An election for the alternative basis of Rent-a-Room relief, or revocation of an election	Within one year after 31 January next following the tax year
Claim for Income Tax relief under the Enterprise Investment Scheme	Within five years after 31 January next following that in which the shares were issued
Declaration by a married couple that their beneficial interest in joint property and the income arising from it are unequal	The date of the declaration which must be sent to the Inland Revenue within 60 days

Chapter 12 – Capital Gains Tax

Claims to the capital loss where the value of an asset becomes negligible	The loss arises on the date of claim although, in practice, a two-year period is allowed from the end of the tax year in which the asset became of negligible value
Claim for the loss on shares that were originally subscribed for in an unquoted trading company to be set against income in the year of loss, or the preceding year	No later than one year after 31 January next following the tax year in which the loss was made
An election for the capital gains on disposals of assets you owned on 31 March 1982 to be worked out by reference to their values on that date, ignoring original costs	Within one year after 31 January next following the tax year in which the first disposal of an asset you owned on 31 March 1982 takes place
Claim for the 6 April 1965 value to be substituted in a calculation of the capital gain arising on the sale of an asset held at that date	No later than one year after 31 January next following the tax year in which the disposal is made
An election to determine which of your homes is to be regarded as your principal residence for Capital Gains Tax purposes	Two years from the date when two or more properties are eligible
Disposal of assets and reinvestment of gain in qualifying company	Within five years after 31 January next following the tax year to which it relates

Claim to roll-over relief on the disposal of business assets	No later than five years after 31 January next following the tax year to which it relates
Claim to a reduction in the deferred gain on assets acquired in the period 31 March 1982 to 5 April 1988	Within one year after 31 January next following the tax year in which the disposal takes place

16

INHERITANCE TAX

Not only might Inheritance Tax be payable on transfers or gifts you make during your lifetime, but it is also due on the value of your estate on death. Husband and wife are treated as separate individuals, and both are entitled to the various exemptions. Inheritance Tax is far from straightforward. What follows is a brief outline. The Tax is administered by the Capital Taxes Office, to whom all Returns and Accounts should be submitted.

Potentially exempt transfers

The most significant feature of Inheritance Tax is the concept of a potentially exempt transfer (PET). This is:

- an outright gift to an individual;
- a gift into an accumulation-and-maintenance settlement;
- a gift into a settlement for the benefit of a disabled person;
- a gift into an interest in possession trust;
- the termination of an interest in possession settlement where the settled property passes to an individual, an accumulation-and-maintenance settlement, or a trust for the benefit of a disabled person.

No tax is payable providing the donor lives for at least seven years after making the gift. A form of tapering relief applies where death occurs within seven years. The amount of Inheritance Tax is then calculated at the rates which apply at the date of death as shown in the following table:

Number of Years between Gift and Death	% of Tax Payable
Not more than 3	100
Between 3 and 4	80
Between 4 and 5	60
Between 5 and 6	40
Between 6 and 7	20

Suppose, however, the PET is within the limit of chargeable transfers taxable at a nil rate. There will then be no benefit from tapering relief as no Inheritance Tax is payable on the PET.

Gifts with reservation

If you make a gift but continue to enjoy some benefit from it, the property or asset you have given away is likely to be treated as yours until either the date when you cease to enjoy any benefit from the gift, or your death. This is a 'gift with reservation'. For example, you give your house to your children but continue to live there, rent free. Your house would then be counted as part of your estate and the seven year period would not start until you either moved home or began to pay a commercial rent.

Lifetime gifts

If you make a gift during your lifetime which is not a potentially exempt transfer it will attract liability to Inheritance Tax at one half of the rates which apply on death. An example of such a lifetime gift is a transfer into a discretionary trust.

Exemptions

The main exemptions applicable to individuals are:

- transfers between husband and wife, during lifetime and on death;

- gifts up to £3,000 in any one tax year. Any part of the exemption which is left over can be carried forward to the following year only. For example, if your total transfers came to £1,200 during 2001/02 you could have given away as much as £4,800 during 2002/03 all within your annual exemption limit. However, if your gifts totalled £3,000 in 2001/02, you would be limited to £3,000 in 2002/03 as well;

- gifts to any one person up to £250 per person in each tax year. Where the total amount given to any one individual exceeds this limit no part comes within this exemption;

- marriage gifts. The amount you can give away in consideration of marriage depends on your relationship to the bride or groom, as follows:

	£
By either parent	5,000
By a grandparent or great-grandparent	2,500
By any other person	1,000

- regular gifts out of income which form part of your normal expenditure;

- gifts to charities and 'qualifying' political parties, both without limit. Both these exceptions apply to lifetime gifts and to bequests on death;

- lump sums paid out of your Pension Scheme on death. The trustees should have discretion over who receives the cash payments.

Business property

Subject to certain conditions, qualifying business assets and interests in businesses qualify for relief for transfers arising either in lifetime or on death. There are two rates:

100% for:

- unincorporated businesses;
- all holdings of unquoted shares in qualifying companies.

50% for:

- shares giving control of a quoted company;
- land, buildings, machinery or plant used in a partnership or controlled company where the transferor is a partner or controlling shareholder.

Unquoted shares include those traded on the Alternative Investment Market (AIM).

Agricultural property

The reliefs applying to agricultural land and holdings are similar to those for business property. Subject to certain minimum ownership and use conditions, the two rates are again:

100% for:

- land and buildings where the transferor has vacant possession, or the right to obtain it, within 12 months;
- agricultural property let for periods exceeding 12 months where the letting commenced on or after 1 September 1995.

50% for:

- other qualifying property.

Trusts

There are special provisions covering the application of Inheritance Tax to different types of Trust. Perhaps the three most common forms of trust are:

- Interest in Possession Trusts where someone is entitled to the trust income as and when it arises. For Inheritance Tax purposes the person so entitled is deemed to own the trust assets personally;

- Discretionary Trusts, where income is distributed at the discretion of the trustees. There are complex rules for computing the liabilities which can arise when assets pass from the trust to beneficiaries. A further charge arises on the assets in the trust on each tenth anniversary from its commencement;

- Accumulation and Maintenance Trusts, which, generally, provide for young members of a family. To qualify under this category the trust must provide that someone will become entitled to either the capital or the income of the trust by the age of 25. Until then no interest in possession must exist. For such qualifying trusts, no charge to Inheritance Tax arises when the beneficiaries become entitled.

Rates of tax

Each taxable gift or transfer is not considered in isolation in calculating how much tax is payable on it. In working out how much is payable, previous taxable transfers are taken into account. This is because the tax due on each chargeable gift or the value of your estate on death is dependent upon the cumulative value of all other chargeable transfers in the seven years leading up to the date of the next chargeable transfer. The rates payable on death from 6 April 2002 are:

Band	Rate
£	%
0–250,000	0
Over 250,000	40

These rates also apply to all lifetime gifts or transfers within three years of death. Inheritance Tax payable on PETS more than three years before but within seven years of death is determined by the first table in this chapter.

The limit of £250,000 on chargeable transfers taxable at a nil rate is increased each year in the same way as the main personal Income Tax allowances.

Illustration

Wendy Brown, a widow, died on 30 September 2002 leaving her entire estate to her daughter. She did not make any gifts in the seven years leading up to her death. Her assets and unpaid bills on her death were:

Assets	Value	
	£	£
Flat	200,000	
Household effects	2,000	
Car	5,000	

Building society account	30,000	
Shares	40,000	
Current account	2,500	
		279,500
Less: Allowable Deductions		
Funeral expenses	920	
Income Tax	500	
Telephone bill	50	
Electricity bill	60	
		1,530
Net Value of Estate		**£277,970**
Inheritance Tax Payable		
On first £250,000		Nil
On next £27,970 at 40%		£11,188
		£11,188

The tax is payable out of Wendy Brown's estate by the executors of her will.

Sales at a loss

Relief is available where certain assets are sold during specified periods after death for less than the valuation at the date of death.

- In the case of land and buildings, the period is four years.
- For quoted securities the time limit is one year.

The relief is available to 'the appropriate person' (the one who pays the tax). All sales by that person in the respective periods must be aggregated. As a result, losses may accordingly be reduced or eliminated by profits so that the relief could be restricted or lost. When this type of relief is due, the net proceeds of sale are substituted for the valuation at death. The Inheritance Tax liability is then recalculated.

Returns

On a death the Return form is made and submitted together with an application for a Grant of:

- Probate where there is a Will; or
- Administration where there is no Will.

The Return must be lodged within 12 months of the date of death. It must include information about previous transfers and gifts which are required to work out the Inheritance Tax payable. You are well advised, therefore, to maintain complete records of your lifetime gifts. Also, to assist your executors you should maintain up-to-date details of all your assets and where the supporting certificates and documents are stored.

Usually it is not necessary to submit a Return where the deceased's estate does not exceed £220,000.

As with your annual Tax Return there are penalties for late Returns, delays, negligence or fraud.

Payment of tax

The persons primarily liable for payment of Inheritance Tax are:

- the transferor in respect of chargeable lifetime gifts;
- the personal representatives on death.

The due dates for payment are:

- for chargeable lifetime gifts – six months after the end of the month in which the gift was made;
- for potentially exempt transfers which become chargeable on death, and the charge on death itself – six months after the end of the month in which the death occurred.

There is an option to pay the tax on certain types of assets by ten equal annual instalments. The first payment is due on the normal due date.

The relevant assets are:

- land and buildings;
- controlling shareholdings;
- unquoted shares, subject to certain conditions;
- businesses.

In the case of lifetime transfers which are, or become, chargeable, the instalment option is only available if the tax is borne by the transferee. Where the asset is sold during the instalment paying period, outstanding instalments become payable immediately.

Interest is payable on Inheritance Tax liabilities from the due date until the date of payment. At the time of going to print the rate of interest is 3%. Where the instalment option is in force, no interest is payable on the outstanding instalments except on:

- land and buildings which do not qualify for business property or agricultural property relief;
- shares and securities in investment companies.

Legacies

Any Inheritance Tax due on a legacy you receive under a will will be accounted for by the executors of the estate before the legacy is paid over to you. You do not pay either Income Tax or Capital Gains Tax on a legacy. It does not need to be reported on your annual Tax Return.

Intestacy

If you die without having made a will your estate will be divided up under the statutory intestacy rules. If you are married and survived by both your spouse and children, your spouse is entitled to a statutory legacy of £125,000. This increases to £200,000 if there are no children but you are survived by specific relatives.

The present intestacy rules for individuals who die domiciled in England or Wales can be summarized as follows:

Unmarried Individual

Survived by	Division of Estate
(1) Children	Shared equally between them
(2) No children but parents	Divided equally between them
(3) Neither children nor parents, but brothers and sisters	Shared equally between them
(4) No children, parents, brothers, sisters but grandparents	Divided equally between them
(5) Only aunts and uncles	Shared equally between them
(6) No relatives as listed above	Estate passes to Crown

Married Individual

Particular Circumstances	Division
(1) Estate amounts to less than £125,000	All to spouse
(2) Estate exceeds £125,000 and there are children	Spouse is entitled to first £125,000 and a life interest in half the remainder. The balance is shared between the children

(3) Estate is worth less than £200,000 and there are no children	All to spouse
(4) Estate comes to more than £200,000, the couple have no children but parents are still alive	Spouse receives first £200,000 and half the remainder absolutely. The parents divide the rest
(5) As in (4) above, parents are dead, but there are brothers and sisters	As in (4) above but the balance is shared between the brothers and sisters instead of the parents
(6) The only survivor is the spouse	All to spouse

The spouse must survive the intestate individual by 28 days to become entitled under the intestacy rules.

In Scotland the intestacy rules have no application to estates of individuals who die domiciled there. Furthermore, a surviving spouse and/or children are entitled to fixed proportions of the moveable estate of the deceased individual. This rule applies whether the deceased died intestate or had made a will.

17

TAX-SAVING HINTS

Saving tax is not always so straightforward as it sounds. To make a meaningful reduction in your annual tax bill will usually necessitate reorganizing your finances and investments. As a general rule opportunities to save tax should not be considered without due regard to other criteria.

First and foremost comes your own personal circumstances. Maybe you are a married man, and your wife has a low taxable income? You know that if you transfer some investments into her own name you can increase her income so she can benefit from her full personal allowance. If you are paying tax at 40% you should consider doing more to utilize both your wife's band of income taxable at 10% and at the lower rates on savings and dividend income. Alternatively, think about holding bank/building society accounts and other investments in your joint names. Either way you should be able to cut the family tax bill, perhaps significantly.

But remember that the investments given to your wife will then belong to her. Most couples will continue to enjoy the benefits from their saving in tax for many years to come. This is not so for everyone – some couples will split up. While no couple ever wants to contemplate that their marriage might break down, the prospect of this happening should, at the very least, be borne in mind in any tax-planning exercise involving a transfer of assets between spouses. The same rule applies if you are thinking about making gifts to your children. They have been known to squander money and subsequently fall out with their parents.

When it comes to investments, remember that you will sometimes need to be locked into an investment for a number of years to benefit from all the tax attractions that go with it. A typical example of this type of investment is a subscription for new shares in a Venture Capital Trust. Examine the merits of any investment from all angles. Sometimes it will be best to steer clear of investments which are inflexible. You could end up endangering your family's financial security. The same applies to those investments which carry a higher degree of risk.

Throughout life, from childhood to retirement, circumstances and priorities change. At every stage it is important to make well-informed decisions to ensure that you and your family are following the best strategies for achieving your goals. When it comes to tax you may need to adjust your finances to take account of future reductions or increases in the various taxes. You should also be ready to respond to any shift in taxation policy following a change in Government. Remember that when you focus on your estate plan it will be the law at some time in the future, when you die, which will determine the tax payable by your executors.

Self-Assessment

- Remember the key dates for Self-Assessment, particularly those for sending back your complete and signed Tax Return. These are 30 September and 31 January after the end of the tax year. You must send your return back by 30 September if you want the Inland Revenue to calculate your tax. The same date applies if you pay tax under PAYE, and want any underpayment of tax collected by an adjustment to your PAYE code number in the following year.
- Do not forget that the second send-back date of 31 January is critical. You must stick to it. Otherwise a fixed penalty will automatically be applied.
- The main dates of the forthcoming annual Self-Assessment calendar are summarized in Table 10 at the end of the book.
- Always answer *'yes'* to question 19 on page 7 of your Tax Return. Any tax overpaid will then be refunded to you. Otherwise it is likely to be kept by the Inland Revenue for set-off against a future tax payment.
- If the amount of any of your sources of income is substantially different compared to the previous year, use the additional information box on page 8 to explain the reason for the change.
- Remember you can amend your Self-Assessment at any time up to the end of 12 months after the normal filing date.
- Keep proper records. You will find it easier to complete your Tax Return fully and accurately. Furthermore, if your tax office decides to enquire into your Tax Return the records you have kept will help you demonstrate that your Return is accurate and complete in all respects. Remember also to keep your records for the right length of time.
- Always pay your tax on time. If you are late in making payment then not only will you be charged interest but you also run the risk of incurring a surcharge.
- If you have overpaid tax, carefully check the Inland Revenue's interest figures on the adjustment required to your Self-Assessment. There are times when the Inland Revenue's computer program does not produce the right calculation. As a result you may not have been given the right amount of tax-free interest on the repayment.

Allowances and reliefs

- Every taxpayer, man or woman, single or married, is entitled to the personal allowance. Married couples should consider transferring their income-producing assets between them to maximize personal allowances and, where possible, the starting and/or savings and basic rate tax bands. Where this is inappropriate, joint ownership might be an alternative.

- Elderly married couples should not forget to consider whether the rules governing the transfer of the married couple's allowance between husband and wife can save them tax.

- Elderly couples need to pay even more care and attention to their respective incomes. They should make sure they do not lose out on the higher personal age and married couple's allowances for pensioners in the 65–74 and over 74 age brackets. They should keep an eye on the annual income limit above which allowances are restricted. It may pay them to shift some of their savings income into tax-free investments such as National Savings or ISAs. By doing so, they may avoid losing some of their age-related allowances.

- Remember that the income limit for the married couple's allowance is by reference to the husband's income. This always applies even if entitlement to this allowance arises because of the wife's age.

- Around each January/February look out for your new PAYE coding notice for the following tax year. Make sure you have been given the right allowances and that any deductions for unpaid tax or benefits-in-kind are correct. Get in touch with your tax office if anything is unclear.

Your job

- The company car continues to be an important part of the remuneration package for many employees. The present system of taxing company cars aims to encourage the use of cleaner cars by linking the tax charge to the exhaust emission of the car. When you come to change your company car it will pay you to look into the CO_2 emission figure of the proposed replacement car. This could save you tax on your company car benefit.

- Do not overlook that there is no tax charge on parking spaces provided at, or near, your work place.

- The cost of petrol for private mileage paid for by your employer is a taxable benefit calculated on fixed scale charges depending upon the cubic capacity of your company car. You will often be better off paying for your own petrol for non-business travel particularly where your private mileage is low.

- Perhaps your employer is paying you a mileage allowance for using your car, motorcycle or bicycle for business. You can claim tax relief on any difference between the amount you receive and the statutory rate.

- You are not taxable on any contributions made by your employer to your pension scheme or your own personal pension policy.

- Think about enquiring whether your employer operates one of the various share, profit sharing and share option schemes all of which have different investment limits and tax relief. Perhaps membership of whatever scheme is on offer from your employer will be an attractive long-term investment with built-in tax advantages.

Value Added Tax

- If your business is not VAT registered, maintain a regular check on your turnover to make sure you are not exceeding the limit for registration.

- Sometimes it pays to apply for voluntary registration. You may be able to reclaim significant amounts of VAT on purchases for and expenses of your business. However, check on your customers to make sure they are VAT registered and will be able to reclaim the VAT charged on your invoices.

- Look into the merits of the Annual or Cash Accounting Schemes if your annual turnover is less than £600,000.

Sole traders

- Do not forget to advise the Inland Revenue as soon as you become self-employed. There is a penalty of £100 if you do not tell them within 3 months of commencement.

- Then think about your accounting date. For the sake of convenience 31 March is an obvious choice as the date coincides with the end of the tax year. Sometimes, however, it is preferable to go with a date early on in the tax year, such as 30 April, as it allows more time to plan for the funding of the tax payable.

- Maintain proper books and records for your business. Make sure they are accurate and always up to date. Avoid using estimates.

- Where appropriate pay your wife a proper and fair salary for the secretarial or other assistance she gives you.

- Consider taking your wife into partnership where she helps you in your business and your annual profits are such that the top slice is taxable at the higher 40% rate.

- Where you incur mixed expenses – part business with the balance private – be careful over the apportionment calculation and only claim the business element as an expense for tax purposes.

- If you are thinking about buying plant and machinery or, for example, a new car, then it may be better to do so towards the end of your accounting year rather than early in the following year. You benefit from the capital allowances due on the expenditure at an earlier date.

- Explore all the options available for claiming tax relief due on a business loss. You may well find that one or other of the different alternative types of loss-relief claim produces a bigger tax repayment for you. In doing your calculations do not overlook the impact of the tax-free repayment supplement paid by the Inland Revenue.

- If your business is booming and is extremely profitable you should seriously think about transferring it to a limited company where you own the shares. This is one of those areas where you should seek professional advice.

- Lastly, always look to the future and plan for your retirement whether you are contemplating a sale of your business or handing it down to the next generation.

Pensions

- Make pension savings play a significant role as part of your overall personal financial planning.

- Pension schemes offer, perhaps, the greatest scope for tax saving and planning which include:

    Replacing your income when you retire
    Tax relief on premiums at your top rate of tax
    No UK tax payable by pension funds
    Tax-free lump sum on retirement
    Death benefits free of Inheritance Tax

- If you are in employment, look into joining your employer's Group or Stakeholder Pension Scheme. Consider topping up the pension benefits under the scheme by the payment of additional voluntary contributions. As an alternative you can pay up to £3,600 per annum into a Stakeholder Scheme providing your salary is not more than £30,000 a year.

- Keep a close eye on your annual earnings for pension purposes. Subject to the annual earnings limit the maximum contributions you can make each year into a personal pension plan are based on the higher of your salary or business profits for that tax year or in any of the five preceding tax years. This rule is of particular value to those in business with fluctuating profits.

- Maybe you are a non-earner, perhaps a person enjoying a career break or a non-earning spouse. You can now pay up to £3,600 gross p.a. into a pension plan. This allowance also extends to children where contributions can be paid for them by their parents or grandparents.

- If you have not been making the maximum contributions into your retirement annuity contract do not forget you are allowed to carry forward the unused relief for up to six years.

- Where you are still paying premiums into a retirement annuity taken out before the beginning of July 1988 it may be better to continue with this policy rather than start a personal pension plan. Do, however, bear in mind the higher annual contribution limits into a personal pension compared with a retirement annuity.

Tax-favoured investments

- Take a look at the investments available from the Department of National Savings where the return is free of both Income Tax and Capital Gains Tax.

- Make sure you are opening the right type of ISA. If you want to invest more than £3,000 in stocks and shares in any one tax year, you must open a maxi ISA. You can only subscribe to one maxi ISA each tax year. You cannot subscribe to a mini ISA and a maxi ISA in the same tax year. You can subscribe to up to three separate mini ISAs investing in each of the three different types of investments (stocks and shares, cash and life assurance) in the same tax year. You must not subscribe to more than one mini ISA investing in the same type of investment in each tax year.

- Continue with your existing TESSA. The interest on your account is tax free and it can run its course under existing rules. When your TESSA matures you can transfer the capital in the account, but not the accumulated interest, into the cash component of an ISA without affecting the amount of new money that can be subscribed to an ISA.

- Although no new money can now be invested into your PEPs, you do not have to terminate any PEPs you hold. They can continue under the present rules with Income Tax and Capital Gains Tax benefits similar to those that you have enjoyed in the past.

- Venture Capital Trusts are tax-efficient vehicles aimed at encouraging investment in unquoted companies in the UK. Bear in mind, therefore, that an investment in a Venture Capital Trust carries a higher degree of risk. The tax benefits for a *'qualifying subscriber'* are:

  20% Income Tax relief on the amount invested up to £100,000
  Deferral of Capital Gains Tax on gains reinvested
  Tax-free income and capital gains

- Investments under the Enterprise Investment Scheme are also high risk with generous tax benefits.

Capital Gains

- Wherever possible try to utilize fully your annual Capital Gains Tax exemption limit. Any part of the limit not used cannot be carried forward to future years.

- Husband and wife each have their own annual exemption limit. They should consider transferring assets between them, either to use up both exemption limits or to realize gains taxed at a lower rate on one spouse compared to the other.

- Do not forget that the excess of your chargeable gains over and above the exemption limit is charged at the tax rates found by adding the excess to your taxable income. By realizing losses you may be able to substantially reduce your Capital Gains Tax liability – particularly if you are a 40% taxpayer.

- Perhaps you have sold some assets and face a substantial Capital Gains Tax bill on the profits realized? Then why not consider investing under the Enterprise Investment Scheme or in Venture Capital Trust Shares? Only the gain, not the sale proceeds, needs to be reinvested.

- Where it is to your advantage, do not overlook making an election for the gains and losses on disposals of assets which you owned on 31 March 1982 to be calculated solely by reference to their market value at that date. The time limit for making the election is two years after the end of the tax year in which the first disposal of an asset you owned on 31 March 1982 takes place.

Your home

- If you have two homes, you are allowed to make an election stipulating which of your homes you want to be regarded as your principal private residence for Capital Gains Tax purposes where the profit on sale is free of tax. Remember that the election must be made within two years from the date when two or more properties are eligible and can subsequently be varied.

- The last three years of ownership of a property, which at some point in time has been your only or main residence, are always treated as though they were occupied as the main residence.

- Where a property that has been let has also been lived in as a main residence there is an additional relief from the taxable gain relating to the let period up to a maximum £40,000.

- Husband and wife should consider owning a second home jointly. This should help reduce the Capital Gains Tax payable on a future sale as they both may be able to take advantage of their own annual exemption limits in working out the tax payable on a profit on a sale.

- If your job takes you away from home for up to four years, your period away from home will still count as if you were in occupation of your main residence.

- It is not uncommon for unmarried couples to own a home each. They may each be able to nominate a main residence for capital gains purposes.

Miscellaneous

- Now that you can no longer get tax relief on mortgage interest to buy your own home, it might be worthwhile to use any spare cash on deposit with a bank or building society to repay some or all of your mortgage.

- Make your charitable donations under the Gift Aid Scheme. Charities can then further benefit by claiming repayment from the Inland Revenue of the tax you deduct and retain at the basic rate. If you are liable to tax at the top rate of 40% you will also profit as you can deduct such payments in working out your annual higher-rate tax liability.

- Non-taxpayers should get the special form so they can receive their bank and building society interest gross, that is with no deduction for tax. Non-taxpayers are most likely to be pensioners, children or dependent married women.

- You would be well advised to look into taking out a loan to assist in financing the purchase of an investment property which you then intend to let out. This way you will be able to claim the annual interest on the borrowing as a deduction against the net rents received from the property.

- If you are letting furnished accommodation in your home, consider whether you can benefit from Rent-a-Room relief. Gross annual rents below £4,250 are tax free.

- Foreign nationals living in the UK should make the most of their non-UK domicile status for tax purposes. Such individuals are not subject to UK taxation on either overseas investment income or capital gains unless the investment income or capital gains are remitted to, or enjoyed in, the UK.

- Grandparents, or other relatives with the means, can fund tax efficiently for school fees and other costs of educating and maintaining children. This is best done via a Trust. The income the Trustees pay out counts as the children's income for tax purposes. They should be able to reclaim all or part of the tax suffered by the Trustees by off-setting it against their personal allowance.

Inheritance Tax

- Remember that gifts and transfers between husbands and wives are exempt from Inheritance Tax.

- Whenever you can afford to do so, make use of the various exemptions detailed in Chapter 16.

- The *'normal expenditure out of income'* exemption is ideal for paying premiums on life policies written in Trust for the next generations. The policy proceeds will pass to them free of tax. This is an effective method of dealing with an Inheritance Tax liability on death which cannot be avoided.

- While both gifts and legacies to charities are exempt for Inheritance Tax purposes, a lifetime gift of cash or shares to a charity can have attractive Income Tax and Capital Gains Tax benefits for the donor.

- Gifts outside the exemptions should be made as early as possible to increase your chances of surviving the seven-year period. Make immediately chargeable gifts – for example to Discretionary Settlements – before potentially exempt transfers.

- Give assets that do not qualify for relief before those that do.

- Gift assets with low values so that the appreciation accrues to the recipient and outside of your estate.

- Make a will. Otherwise your estate will devolve under the intestacy laws and not in a way that you want. Keep your will up to date.

- Consider restricting chargeable legacies for the next generations to the nil rate band, leaving the rest of your estate to your spouse. He or she can then make gifts and hopefully survive a further seven years.

- Do not waste your nil rate band. Even if you want to leave everything to your spouse, ask about Discretionary Wills. The potential saving in tax for the next generations is significant.

- Where possible look into rearranging your affairs to take advantage of the business or agricultural property reliefs.

- In the two years after death, consider the use of a Deed of Variation in order to utilize any available exemptions which would otherwise be lost.

TABLES

TABLE 1

INLAND REVENUE EXPLANATORY BOOKLETS

No.	Title
IR 1	Extra Statutory Concessions
IR 14/15	Construction Industry Scheme
IR 20	Residents and Non-Residents – Liability to Tax in the United Kingdom
IR 33	Income Tax and School Leavers
IR 34	Pay As You Earn
IR 37	Appeals against Tax, NICs, SSP and SMP
IR 40	Conditions for getting a Sub-Contractor's Tax Certificate
IR 41	Income Tax and Jobseekers
IR 45	What to do about Tax when Someone Dies
IR 56	Employed or Self-Employed? A Guide for Tax and National Insurance
IR 60	Income Tax and Students
IR 64	Giving to Charity by Businesses
IR 65	Giving to Charity by Individuals
IR 68	Accrued Income Scheme: Taxing Securities on Transfer
IR 72	Investigations: The Examination of Business Accounts
IR 73	Inland Revenue Investigations: How Settlements are Negotiated
IR 78	Looking to the future: Tax Reliefs to help you save for retirement
IR 87	Letting and your Home
IR 90	Tax Allowances and Reliefs
IR 95	Approved Profit-Sharing Schemes – An Outline for Employees
IR 97	Approved SAYE Share Option Schemes – An Outline for Employees Schemes
IR 101	Approved Company Share Option Plans – An Outline for Employees
IR 110	A Guide for People with Savings
IR 115	Tax and Childcare
IR 116	Guide for Sub-Contractors with Tax Certificates
IR 117	Guide for Sub-Contractors with Registration Cards
IR 119	Tax Relief for Vocational Training
IR 120	You and the Inland Revenue (National Insurance Contributions Office)
IR 121	Income Tax and Pensioners
IR 122	Volunteer Drivers
IR 123	Mortgage Interest Relief – Buying Your Home
IR 124	Using Your Own Vehicle for Work
IR 131	Inland Revenue Statements of Practice
IR 134	Income Tax and Relocation Packages
IR 136	Income Tax and Company Vans

TABLE 1

IR 137	The Enterprise Investment Scheme
IR 138	Living or Retiring Abroad? A guide to UK tax on your UK income and pension
IR 139	Income from Abroad? A guide to UK tax on overseas income
IR 140	Non-Resident Landlords, their Agents and Tenants
IR 141	Open Government
IR 143	Income Tax and Redundancy
IR 144	Income Tax and Incapacity Benefit
IR 145	Low Interest Loans Provided by Employers: A Guide for Employees
IR 150	Taxation of Rents – A Guide to Property Income
IR 152	Trusts: An Introduction
IR 153	Tax Exemption for Sickness or Unemployment Insurance Payments
IR 155	PAYE Settlement Agreements
IR 160	Inland Revenue Enquiries under Self-Assessment
IR 161	Tax Relief for Employees' Business Travel
IR 162	A Better Approach to Local Office Enquiry Work Under Self-Assessment
IR 167	Charter for Inland Revenue Taxpayers
IR 169	Venture Capital Trusts (VCTs) – A Brief Guide
IR 170	Blind Person's Allowance
IR 171	Income Tax: A Guide for People With Children
IR 172	Income Tax and Company Cars
IR 176	Tax, National Insurance Contributions and Green Travel
IR 177	Share Incentive Plans and Your Entitlement to Benefits
IR 178	Giving Shares and Securities to Charity
SA/BK3	Self-Assessment – A Guide to Keeping Records for the Self-Employed
SA/BK4	Self-Assessment – A General Guide to Keeping Records
SA/BK6	Self-Assessment – Penalties for Late Tax Returns
SA/BK7	Self-Assessment – Surcharges for Late Payment of Tax
SA/BK8	Self-Assessment – Your Guide
480	Expenses and Benefits: A Tax Guide
CGT 1	Capital Gains Tax: A Quick Guide
IHT 2	Inheritance Tax on Lifetime Gifts
IHT 3	Inheritance Tax: An Introduction
IHT 14	Inheritance Tax: The Personal Representative's Responsibilities

TABLE 2

FLAT-RATE ALLOWANCES FOR SPECIAL CLOTHING AND THE UPKEEP OF TOOLS – 2002/03

(1) Fixed rate for all occupations

	£
Agricultural	70
Forestry	70
Quarrying	70
Brass and copper	100
Precious metals	70
Textile prints	60
Food	40
Glass	60
Railways (non-crafts people)	70
Uniformed prison officers	55
Uniformed bank employees	40
Uniformed police officers up to and including chief inspector	55
Uniformed fire fighters and fire officers	60

(2) Variable rate depending on category of occupation

Seamen	130/135
Iron mining	75/100
Iron and steel	45/60/120
Aluminium	45/60/100/130
Engineering	45/60/100/120
Shipyards	45/60/75/115
Vehicles	40/60/105
Particular engineering	45/60/100/120
Constructional engineering	45/60/75/115
Electrical and electricity supply	25/90
Textiles	60/85
Clothing	30/45
Leather	40/55
Printing	30/70/105
Building materials	40/55/85
Wood and furniture	45/75/90/115
Building	40/55/85/105
Heating	70/90/100
Public service	40/55
Healthcare	45/60/70/110

Note

The allowances are only available to manual workers who have to bear the cost of upkeep of tools and special clothing. Other employees, such as office staff, cannot claim them.

TABLE 3

VAT NOTICES AND LEAFLETS

No.	Title
48	Extra Statutory Concessions
700	The VAT Guide
700/1	Should I be Registered for VAT?
700/11	Cancelling your Registration
700/12	Filling in your VAT Return
700/15	The Ins and Outs of VAT
700/21	Keeping Records and Accounts
700/41	Late Registration: Penalty
700/42	Misdeclaration Penalties
700/43	Default Interest
700/45	How to Correct VAT Errors and make Adjustments or Claims
700/50	Default Surcharge
700/51	VAT Enquiries Guide
727	Retail Schemes
731	Cash Accounting
732	Annual Accounting
733	Flat Rate Scheme for Small Businesses
930	What if I don't pay?
989	Visits by Customs and Excise Officers
999	Catalogue of Publications
1000	Complaints and Putting Things Right

TABLE 4

RATES OF NATIONAL INSURANCE CONTRIBUTIONS FOR 2002/03

CLASS 1 Contributions for Employees

	Standard Rate		Contracted Out	
	On First £89.00	On Remainder	On First £89.00	On Remainder
Contributions levied on all weekly earnings if they reach £89.00				
but do not exceed £585.00	NIL	10%	NIL	8.4%
If weekly earnings exceed £585.00	No Additional Contributions		No Additional Contributions	

Reduced Rate for Married Women and Widows with a Valid Election Certificate	3.85%
	£
Men over 65 and Women over 60	Nil
Earnings Threshold — Weekly	89.00
— Monthly	385.00
— Annually	4,615.00
Upper Earnings Limit — Weekly	585.00
— Monthly	2,535.00
— Annually	30,420.00

CLASS 2 Contributions for the Self-Employed

Weekly flat rate	2.00
Small earnings exception	4,615.00

CLASS 3 Voluntary Contributions

Weekly rate	6.85

CLASS 4 Contributions for the Self-Employed 7% of profits between £4,615 and £30,420

TABLE 5

NATIONAL INSURANCE EXPLANATORY LEAFLETS

CA01	National Insurance Contributions for Employees
CA02	National Insurance Contributions for Self-Employed People with Small Earnings
CA04	National Insurance Contributions: Class 2 and Class 3 Direct Debit – The Easier Way to Pay
CA07	National Insurance Contributions – Unpaid and Late-Paid Contributions
CA08	National Insurance Contributions – Voluntary Contributions
CA09	National Insurance Contributions for Widows or Widowers
CA10	National Insurance Contributions for Divorcees
CA12	Training for Further Employment and Your NI Record
CA13	National Insurance Contributions for Married Women with Reduced Elections
CA 17	Employees' Guide to Minimum Contributions
CWL 2	National Insurance Contributions for Self-Employed People: Class 2 and Class 4

TABLE 6

Social Security Benefits

Taxable
Incapacity Benefit after the first 28 weeks (1)
Industrial Death Benefit Pensions
Invalid Care Allowance (1)
Jobseeker's Allowance
Retirement Pension (1)
Statutory Maternity Pay
Statutory Sick Pay
Widowed Parent's Allowance (1)
Bereavement Allowance

Non-taxable
Incapacity Benefit for the first 28 weeks
Income Support
Maternity Allowance
Child Benefit
Child's Special Allowance
Guardian's Allowance
One-Parent Benefit
Christmas Bonus for Pensioners
Industrial Injury Benefits
War Disablement Benefits
Disability Living Allowance
Disabled Person's Tax Credit
Bereavement Payment
Earnings Top-Up
Working Families' Tax Credit
Housing Benefit
Jobfinder's Grant
War Widow's, Widower's or Dependant's Pension
Social Fund Payments
Attendance Allowance
Council Tax Benefit
Redundancy Payment
Vaccine Damage (Lump Sum)
Television Licence Payment
Winter Fuel Payment

Note
(1) Child dependency additions to these benefits are not taxable.

TABLE 7

Rates of Main Social Security Benefits for 2002/03

	Weekly Rate from 08.04.2002 Onwards £
Taxable	
Retirement pensions	
Single person	75.00
Married couple's	
both contributors – each	75.00
wife not contributor – addition	45.20
Age addition (over 80) – each	0.25
Bereavement benefits	
Bereavement allowance/widow's pension – maximum	75.50
Widowed parent's allowance	75.50
Jobseeker's allowance	
Under age 18	32.50
Age 18 to 24	42.70
Age 25 or over	53.95
Incapacity benefit	
Long-term	70.95
Increase for age: higher rate	14.90
lower rate	7.45
Short-term (under pension age) lower rate	53.50
higher rate	63.25
(over pension age) lower rate	68.05
higher rate	70.95
Statutory sick pay	
Standard rate (weekly earnings threshold £75)	75.00
Statutory maternity pay	
Lower rate (weekly earnings threshold £75)	75.00
Non-taxable	
Maternity allowance	
Standard rate	75.00
Child benefit	
Only or eldest child (couple)	15.75
Each other child	10.55
Only or eldest child (lone parent)	17.55
Attendance allowance	
Higher rate	56.25
Lower rate	37.65

TABLE 8

SCOPE OF LIABILITY TO INCOME TAX OF EARNINGS

		Duties of employment performed wholly or partly in the UK		Duties of employment performed wholly outside the UK
		In the UK	Outside the UK	
Foreign emoluments[1]	Employee resident and ordinarily resident in the UK	Liable	Liable	Liable if received in the UK
	Resident but not ordinarily resident	Liable	Liable if received in the UK	Liable if received in the UK
	Not resident	Liable	Not liable	Not liable
Other earnings	Resident and ordinarily resident	Liable	Liable	Liable
	Resident but not ordinarily resident	Liable	Liable if received in the UK	Liable if received in the UK
	Not resident	Liable	Not liable	Not liable

Notes
(1) 'Foreign emoluments' is the term to mean the earnings of someone who is not domiciled in the UK and whose employer is not resident in, and is resident outside, the UK.

TABLE 9

Capital Gains Tax – The Indexation Allowance: April 1998

Starting Months and Years for Indexation

	1982	1983	1984	1985	1986	1987
January	–	0.968	0.872	0.783	0.689	0.626
February	–	0.960	0.865	0.769	0.683	0.620
March	1.047	0.956	0.859	0.752	0.681	0.616
April	1.006	0.929	0.834	0.716	0.665	0.597
May	0.992	0.921	0.828	0.708	0.662	0.596
June	0.987	0.917	0.823	0.704	0.663	0.596
July	0.986	0.906	0.825	0.707	0.667	0.597
August	0.985	0.898	0.808	0.703	0.662	0.593
September	0.987	0.889	0.804	0.704	0.654	0.588
October	0.977	0.883	0.793	0.701	0.652	0.580
November	0.967	0.876	0.788	0.695	0.638	0.573
December	0.971	0.871	0.789	0.693	0.632	0.574

	1988	1989	1990	1991	1992	1993
January	0.574	0.465	0.361	0.249	0.199	0.179
February	0.568	0.454	0.353	0.242	0.193	0.171
March	0.562	0.448	0.339	0.237	0.189	0.167
April	0.537	0.423	0.300	0.222	0.171	0.156
May	0.531	0.414	0.288	0.218	0.167	0.152
June	0.525	0.409	0.283	0.213	0.167	0.153
July	0.524	0.408	0.282	0.215	0.171	0.156
August	0.507	0.404	0.269	0.213	0.171	0.151
September	0.500	0.395	0.258	0.208	0.166	0.146
October	0.485	0.384	0.248	0.204	0.162	0.147
November	0.478	0.372	0.251	0.199	0.164	0.148
December	0.474	0.369	0.252	0.198	0.168	0.146

	1994	1995	1996	1997	1998
January	0.151	0.114	0.083	0.053	0.019
February	0.144	0.107	0.078	0.049	0.014
March	0.141	0.102	0.073	0.046	0.011
April	0.128	0.091	0.066	0.040	–
May	0.124	0.087	0.063	0.036	–
June	0.124	0.085	0.063	0.032	–
July	0.129	0.091	0.067	0.032	–
August	0.124	0.085	0.062	0.026	–
September	0.121	0.080	0.057	0.021	–
October	0.120	0.085	0.057	0.019	–
November	0.119	0.085	0.057	0.019	–
December	0.114	0.079	0.053	0.016	–

TABLE 10

MAIN DATES OF THE SELF-ASSESSMENT CALENDAR
6 APRIL 2003 – 5 APRIL 2004

Date	What happens	Who is affected
6 April 2003	2002/03 Tax Returns sent out by the Inland Revenue.	Taxpayers who need to fill in an annual Tax Return.
31 July 2003	Second payment on account due for 2002/03.	Those taxpayers who make regular half-yearly payments on account.
	Second £100 penalty levied for failing to submit a 2001/02 Tax Return.	Taxpayers who have not yet completed and sent back their 2001/02 Tax Returns.
	Further automatic 5% surcharge on tax still outstanding for 2001/02.	Late payers of tax still due for 2001/02.
30 September 2003	First filing deadline for completing and returning 2002/03 Tax Returns.	Taxpayers who want the Inland Revenue to: • calculate their tax for 2002/03 • collect tax owing for 2002/03 of less than £2,000 through their code number in 2004/05.
31 January 2004	Filing deadline for 2002/03 Tax Returns.	Taxpayers sent a 2002/03 Tax Return.
	Payment date for the balance of tax due for 2002/03 and the first payment on account for 2003/04.	Taxpayers who need to settle either of these liabilities.
1 February 2004	First penalty of £100 charged for the late filing of a 2002/03 Tax Return.	Taxpayers who were sent a 2002/03 Tax Return.
28 February 2004	First automatic 5% surcharge imposed for failing to pay tax due for 2002/03.	Late payers of tax for 2002/03.

2003 BUDGET MEASURES

2003/04 Personal Allowances

		£
Personal	– (age under 65)	4,615
	– (age 65–74)	6,600
	– (age 75 and over)	6,720
Married couples	– (born before 6 April 1935 and aged less than 75)	*5,565
	– (age 75 and over)	*5,635
	– (minimum amount)	*2,150
Income limit for age-related allowances		18,300
Relief for blind person (each)		1,510

* Indicates allowances where tax relief is restricted to 10%.

Tax Rates and Bands for 2003/04

Band of Taxable Income	Rate of Tax	Tax on Band	Cumulative Tax
£	%	£	£
0– 1,960	10	196.00	196.00
1,961–30,500	22	6,278.80	6,474.80
over 30,500	40		

Rates of National Insurance Contributions for 2003/04

CLASS I Contributions for Employees

		Standard Rate	Contracted Out
Contributions levied on all weekly earnings above but do not exceed	£89.00 £595.00	11%	9.4%
If weekly earnings exceed	£595.00	1%	1%

Reduced Rate for Married Women and Widows with a Valid Election Certificate			
if weekly earnings exceed	£595.00		4.85%
			1%
Men over 65 and Women over 60			Nil
Employee's Earnings Threshold	• Weekly		£89.00
	• Monthly		£385.00
	• Annually		£4,615.00

Upper Earnings Limit	• Weekly	£595.00
	• Monthly	£2,576.00
	• Annually	£30,940.00

CLASS 2 Contributions for the Self-Employed
Weekly flat rate £2.00
Small Earnings Exception £4,615.00

CLASS 3 Voluntary Contributions
Weekly rate £6.95

CLASS 4 Contributions for the Self-Employed
On profits between £4,615 and £30,940 8%
If profits exceed £30,940 1%

Employment Benefits – Minor Measures

Long Service Awards

Employers can currently make a non-cash award to an employee tax-free in recognition of long service. The employee must have a minimum of 20 years service with the employer and the gift can be valued up to £20 per year of service. Additional gifts can be made at 10 yearly intervals. It is proposed that the £20 limit be increased to £50 for each year of service.

Annual Party

Generally, a party or celebration paid for by an employer is exempt from tax where the cost is no more than £75 per head. It is intended to double this exemption to £150 per head.

Third Party Gifts

Employees receiving non-cash gifts from third parties can receive them free of tax provided the value is £150 or less. This amount is to be increased to £250.

Cycle to Work Days – Meals and Refreshments

The requirement to report a benefit in kind when an employer provides meals or refreshments as an incentive to employees to take part in cycle to work days was removed from 6 April 2002. The legislation limits the number of occasions on which an employer can provide such meals to six per year. It is proposed that this limit should be removed.

Employer Provided Vans

The Government has announced a forthcoming consultation on proposals to reform the tax treatment of employer provided vans. This will affect employees having a van available for their private use and employers who currently bear Class 1A National Insurance on the taxable benefit.

At present, a flat-rate charge of £500 (£350 for vans more than four years old) applies where the employee has exclusive use of the van, including the provision of any private fuel. The charge is divided equally between employees who share the same van.

Payments by Employers Towards Incidental Homeworking Costs

Employees are normally charged income tax on payments made by their employer towards additional household costs as a result of working from home under agreed flexible working arrangements. This measure means that employers can contribute towards some or all of the incidental household costs incurred by employees working at home without giving rise to a tax charge or incurring liability to National Insurance Contributions.

From 6 April 2003, employers will be able to pay up to £2 per week (£104 per year) without supporting evidence of the costs incurred by the employee. If this limit is exceeded, the exemption still applies but the employer will be required to provide supporting evidence that the payment wholly relates to additional household expenses incurred by the employee in carrying out duties at home.

Financial Support to Adopters

Payments by local authorities and adoption agencies to adopters are currently exempt from tax under an Extra Statutory Concession given by the Inland Revenue. This does not, however, apply to financial support paid under the new Adoption and Children Act 2002 so new legislation is being put in place such that the tax exemption of adoption support should have a statutory footing.

The new measure takes effect from the 6 April 2003, although payments under previous legislation continue to be tax-free before this date.

Foster Carers

A new tax relief is to be introduced for foster carers consisting of two elements:

- Where gross receipts from foster care do not exceed an individual limit in a year, the carer will be exempt from tax on foster-care income;
- Where gross receipts exceed the limit, foster carers will be able to opt for a simplified method of calculating their taxable profits.

The individual limit will comprise a fixed amount of £10,000 per residence for a full year and an additional amount of £200 per week for each child aged under eleven increasing to £250 per week for children aged over ten.

The relief will be introduced from 6 April 2003 and applies solely to income obtained from the provision of foster care.

Domestic Workers

The Chancellor has announced provisions to close a tax avoidance device whereby domestic workers, such as nannies or butlers, operate through a service company rather than be treated as directly employed by the person to whom they provide their services. The change will affect income received in relation to services provided after 9 April 2003 and there will also be an amendment to the National Insurance regulations to bring them into line with tax.

The proposed measure extends the current intermediaries legislation which is limited to those providing personal services to a business carried on by a client. Domestic workers who provide services through an intermediary, such as a company, will now be brought within the scope of the legislation. This ensures that workers who would be treated as employees if engaged directly rather than through a company cannot avoid paying tax and National Insurance in the same way as other employees.

Pension Scheme Earnings Limit

Pension contributions for members of occupational pension schemes established on or after 14 March 1989, and for members joining schemes established before that date on or after 1 June 1989, are restricted to those based on a maximum annual earnings limit. This earnings cap is increased from £97,200 to £99,000 from 6 April 2003. It also applies to all personal pension schemes.

Employee Share Schemes

All employers who operate an employee share scheme and their employees who benefit from such schemes are likely to be affected by a number of anti-avoidance, reform and simplification measures announced in the Budget. Of particular interest are:

- Employees who are members of either a Share Incentive or a Save-As-You-Earn Plan are exempt from the payment of tax and National Insurance Contributions if their participation ends through redundancy, injury, disability or retirement.

  From 9 April 2003 the same treatment is extended to employees who are members of a Company Share Option Plan and leave employment in similar circumstances.

- Currently, employees can only purchase partnership shares in a Share Incentive Plan through deductions of up to £125 or 10%, whichever is lower, from their monthly salary. An amendment to these rules will allow employees to purchase up to the annual limit of partnership shares at any time within the year. Dividends of up to £1,500 each year received by employees on Share Incentive Plan shares can be reinvested into more shares. At present these shares must be held for 3 years to qualify for tax reliefs. The holding period for dividend shares is being aligned to the holding period for base shares. These measures are operative from the date that the Finance Bill receives Royal Assent.

- Employees must refund to their employer the Income Tax on their share-option gains within 30 days of exercising the option. Missing this deadline can lead to an effective surcharge of 16% on the gain. From 9 April 2003 this deadline is being extended to 90 days. From an appointed day after Royal Assent to the Finance Bill the National Insurance rules will be changed so that this 90 day period will also apply to National Insurance liabilities where the tax has not been reimbursed.

Life Insurance – Policyholder Taxation

The Finance Bill 2003 will contain legislation ending four anomalies that give rise to inappropriate charges to tax and closing three loopholes that lead to tax avoidance.

Group Life Policies

A group life policy is one that insures the lives of a group of individuals and pays benefits on each death. Multiple payments of the death benefit can lead to unintended tax charges on either the insured members or the policyholder.

A measure, effective not only from 9 April 2003 but also retrospectively, will ensure that there will be no tax charge on death benefits paid under group life protection policies so long as they meet certain conditions. Insurers and policyholders also have until 5 April 2004 to vary existing policies that do not presently meet all of the conditions.

This should help partnerships, professional associations and members of trade unions with group life policies.

Life Insurance – Exceptional risk of disability

A life insurance policy will not lose its qualifying status when an insurer removes:

- A charge on the policy proceeds; or
- A premium loading

that was originally imposed because the insured person then had an exceptional risk of suffering a disability or critical illness. This relieving provision is fully retrospective.

Maturity Options

Under current law there is no tax charge when a policy matures if the policyholder exercises an option to re-invest all the proceeds of the maturing policy with the same insurer in a new policy.

This rule ends for policies maturing on or after 9 April 2003. The gain on maturity of the first policy is immediately taxable.

Child Trust Fund

The Child Trust Fund is a new initiative intended to strengthen financial education, promote positive attitudes to saving and ensure that all children, regardless of family background, will benefit from access to a stock of financial assets when they start their adult lives. It will be introduced to children across the United Kingdom by:

- Providing an initial endowment at birth for every child of £250, increasing to £500 for children from lower-income families who also qualify for full Child Tax Credit;
- Allowing additional contributions to be made by parents, family members and friends, up to an annual limit of £1,000.
- Being accessible when children reach 18 years of age, whereupon there will be no restriction to the use of all assets;
- Being delivered through open market competition with accounts expected to be available by 2005.

Capital Allowances

The 100% first-year allowance for investments by small businesses in information and communications technology and energy-saving technologies has been extended for a further twelve months to 31 March 2004.

Value Added Tax

The Value Added Tax registration threshold is increased with effect from 10 April 2003 from annual taxable turnover of £55,000 to £56,000. The cancellation of registration limit goes up from £53,000 to £54,000.

The measures introduced last year to assist small- and medium-sized enterprises to reduce their VAT administration burden, have been amended from 10 April 2003 as follows:

- The VAT exclusive turnover ceiling for entry into the flat-rate scheme rises from £100,000 to £150,000 and the overall turnover ceiling from £125,000 to £187,500.
- The taxable turnover threshold for businesses to enter the annual accounting regime immediately, rather than having to wait until a year's VATable trading has been completed, rises from £100,000 to £150,000.

A number of measures have been introduced to improve compliance and improve the collection of VAT. These include:

- The introduction of a one-off incentive scheme to allow businesses to notify Customs and Excise of their liability to register outside the statutory time limits without incurring a belated notification penalty. However, all arrears of tax will have to be paid in full. This scheme will run from 10 April to 30 September 2003.

- An extension to the evidence required to support a claim for the repayment of input tax where the claimant does not hold a valid VAT invoice. This measure only applies to businesses in trade sectors dealing with computers, telephones (and their respective related equipment), alcohol products and road fuel. This measure will come into effect on 16 April 2003.

Capital Gains Tax

The Capital Gains Tax annual exemption limit is increased to £7,900.

The definition of 'business asset' has been widened to enable more individuals to benefit from the generous asset taper relief. These rules have previously been relaxed and it should be noted that unexpected results can occur where an asset is owned for a time period that straddles a change in the legislation.

From 6 April 2004 an asset owned by an individual will qualify as a business asset for periods that it is used wholly or partly for the purpose of a trade carried on by:

- Any individual, trustee or personal representative of a deceased person

- Any partnership which has an individual as a member or whose members include any person acting in the cpacity of a trustee of a settlement or as a personal representative

- A partnership whose members include a qualifying company by reference to the owner of the asset

- A partnership whose members include a company which belongs to a trading group whose holding company is a qualifying company by reference to the owner of the asset.

From 6 April 2000 all unlisted trading companies have been 'qualifying companies'. For periods up to 5 April 2004 the asset held by the individual will need to be used in a trade carried on by that individual or used in the trade of a qualifying company.

Inheritance Tax

From 6 April 2003 the nil-rate band increases from £250,000 to £255,000.